Transformation of the Heart:

A Contemplative Practice

GINA ANDERSON

Transformation of the Heart:
A Contemplative Practice

GINA ANDERSON

Island Press
Vashon Island, Washington

Copyright 2011 by Gina Anderson

All rights reserved. No part of this publication may be reproduced, stored in a retrieval system, or transmitted, in any form or by any means, electronic, mechanical, photocopying, or otherwise, without the prior written permission of the author.

Icon written by Br. Claude Lane, Order of St. Benedict,
Mount Angel Abbey and Seminary; St. Benedict, Oregon

Comments and inquiries regarding this book may be sent to the author at
ganderson@communityactivators.com

Editor: Christine Dubois
Proofreader: Nancy Morgan, Eagle Eye Proofreading & Editing
Book Layout and Design: Gretchen Flickinger, Ink Plus Inc.
Book Production: Natalie Kosovac, Natfly Productions

This book is available for purchase at Island Press, Amazon.com, Barnesandnoble.com, and through your favorite bookstores.

ISBN: 978-0-9773877-3-1

Library of Congress Control Number: 2010917055

Published by
Island Press
P.O. Box 328
Vashon, WA 98070

Contents

Acknowledgements 7
Foreword 9
Introduction 11
Definitions 19

Section One Overview:
The Desire to Love Jesus 25
Chapter One — An Embrace with God 29
Chapter Two — The Greatest Commandment 35
Chapter Three — Drawn to a Divine Proclamation 39
Chapter Four — "Little Spirit of Jesus" 45

Section Two Overview:
Healing Ministries of God's Love 49
Chapter Five — Transformation of the Heart
    Healing Paradigm 53
Chapter Six — How to Begin 69
Chapter Seven — Two Personal Healing Stories 75
Chapter Eight — Healing Hands Prayer 81

Section Three Overview: The Fulfillment of Desire:
Oneness with God 91
Chapter Nine — What is Gained and What is Lost 95
Chapter Ten — The Eternal Nature of God's Love 101
Chapter Eleven — A Glimpse of the Kingdom of Heaven 121

About the Author 133

*Then Jesus said to the Jews who had believed in him,
if you continue in my word, you are truly my disciples;
and you will know the truth,
and the truth will make you free* (John 8:31-32).

Acknowledgements

I give thanks to God who invites all to the table of love and forgiveness. I trust that God's grace and love are ever present in all people all of the time. May this work inspired in me touch your heart and desire to love the Lord.

Thank you and special blessings to everyone who helped create this book and support me along the way.

Editor Christine Dubois, who smoothed out the rough edges of my prose and made the meaning clearer. Thank you for your questions and your persistence.

Graphic Designer Gretchen Flickinger, whose eye for design and layout keeps these pages simple and clear.

Nancy Morgan, master proofreader, whose eye for consistency and detail also brings ease to the reader.

Natalie Kosovac, Natfly Productions, who brought the artistry of book production.

My loving family . . . Bruce, who loves and guides me as only a beloved husband can; and Izak and Bria, our young adult children, who at times did chores while I prayed and wrote. Izak reminded me once that God was not a chore (I think he felt I should be doing a little more of Martha's work). Bria could often be found in the kitchen baking a Sunday pie—to raise money for peace in the world, or to feed family and friends.

Fr. Jerome Young, O.S.B., who offered me spiritual direction for ten years, witnessed the gifts of the Holy Spirit in me and taught me humility of spirit in receiving the Lord's merciful love.

To my special women friends—Carolyn Carlson, Therese DesCamp, Annie Geddes, and Cathryn MacNaughten—who laugh with me, accept me as I am, and bring me gifts of counsel, prayer, and friendship.

To Sister Peg Murphy, who has supported me with counsel in parish ministries as well as Transformation of the Heart retreats, held at Catherine Place, an Oasis for Women in Tacoma, Washington.

I dedicate this small book of my love for Jesus to the Benedictine monks and priests at Mount Angel Abbey and Seminary in Oregon—who pray without ceasing and welcome all with the hospitality of Christ. I am in much gratitude for the Oblate Program, and for Fr. Pius X Harding's leadership in my ongoing formation as an Oblate.

Foreword

Early in the winter of 2006, I was fortunate to meet Gina Anderson. She ostensibly came to attend a class I was teaching on contemplative healing prayer, but I soon discovered that her depth and prayerful connection to God were teaching me.

Gina became a beloved friend as we continued to connect regularly in prayer. She organized a small prayer group that met by phone once a week, initially to pray for a dear friend of hers who was gravely ill. Gradually this small circle of women became a place of major spiritual support for me as we all shared the joys and griefs of our lives as well as our spiritual openings and times of walking through spiritual desert. As I got to know her better, I came to recognize how deeply her life reflects the exceptional nature of God's absolute and unconditional love for all.

As Gina shares her remarkable story of healing and of grace in this book, we learn how she opened herself "during a time of great trial" to the forces and care of the Beloved, and we are privileged to witness her awakenings as the depths of her prayer life become illuminated. We notice her gift of courage to go deep and ever deeper into this life of prayer that seeks always to discern the subtle breath of the holy and the mystical.

As you will see, Gina speaks to God with a boldness and courage born of true humility and love. Her courageous and ceaseless journey of living from God's holy work in her soul is revealed in the unfolding nuances of her daily life. Her fearlessness in the face of great difficulties and disappointments can become a nectar of encouragement for those of us who may fear to look at our own weaknesses, fears, and transgressions with a bold and naked eye, yet one that is as compassionate and merciful as the clear-seeing of Jesus.

It is the direct realization of the enormity of God's love for each individual that is at the core of Gina's healing work. On her path, accepting God's love comes first, followed by the work of our spirit to reconcile and to forgive. As you immerse yourself in Transformation of the Heart, you may find that her stories open you more fully to the grace of God, which can move you ever deeper into this same true knowing of God's abiding, unending love. Gina urges us to live into this understanding, encouraging our hearts to open continuously and ever wider to this holy gift.

This is a work to be read slowly and with a prayerful heart. The unpacking of Gina's spiritual journey cannot be hurried or glossed over. In order to penetrate the depths of Transformation of the Heart, it must be unfurled with careful attention, and time for your own understanding. Her work draws us to a deeper understanding of God's presence, and action within that is the essence of contemplative prayer.

In knowing Gina, I have the advantage of being able to hear her speak her prayers aloud. Listening to the flowing cadence of her words is much like being wrapped in a thick and treasured family quilt when you've just come in from the cold. Though you, the reader, cannot hear the grace and sweetness of her spoken word, what she has written has the power to convey a patient sensitivity and passion for God that is so all-encompassing, your heart can be thrilled and put at ease at the same time.

What I have been blessed to come to know in friendship, may you now be blessed to meet in these pages.

Ann Geddes
Novato, California
July 19, 2011

Ann is a Spiritual Director and teaches Contemplative Healing Prayer.

Introduction

*I am my beloved's, and his desire is for me.
Come, my beloved, let us go forth into the fields,
and lodge in the villages; let us go out early to the vineyards,
and see whether the vines have budded,
whether the grape blossoms have opened
and the pomegranates are in bloom.
There I will give you my love.*
Book of The Song of Solomon 7:10-12

Perhaps you have picked up this book because you are seeking healing or you sense a longing to love that is not yet fulfilled in your spirit.

My heart's awakening to the desire to love the Lord with all of my heart, my spirit, and my mind is the same love that transformed my heart and soul and draws me to write these lessons and blessings of God's love. I pray that what is written will open your heart to further love the Lord and that in his grace, your heart will be transformed into a heart of love, peace, and joy.

What is the nature of human existence, if it is not to love the Lord God with all of our heart, our spirit, and our strength—and through this love, to love one another? The purpose of this book is to awaken in the reader love and the desire to love the Lord Jesus Christ. Through this desire, our deepest longing to be near the Lord is touched by grace. What is the meaning of the desire to love, and what healing happens in the presence of God's grace?

This book is a glimpse into these mysteries of God's love.

This book frames the journey of heart where the Lord's gift—our longing or desire to love him—is nurtured by our participation and our own will to love. The heart's journey to wholeness is accomplished in love given and received in the arms of Christ—where grace is the antidote that brings healing to the heart. Guilt, remorse, and the anguish caused by sin done to us by others are lifted from our heart—and our heart's healing is the centerpiece from which all else flows to the body, mind, spirit, and soul.

There are three sections included in the book that illustrate the depth and process of the Transformation of the Heart journey. Themes threaded throughout each section include Scripture, personal story, blessings of God's love in poetry, wisdom of God's lessons of healing gained during my healing journey, and wisdom of other authors. Transformation of the Heart is a way to heal through conversion of sin, leading the heart to peace and love made manifest.

Section One is about the opening of your heart to Jesus' desire to love you, and to your desire to love Jesus. This is the foundation for the work of the heart's journey to transformation. We know that our desire to love is a gift from the Lord, and that Jesus first loved us. This desire grows in us until the day of our death when eternal life is upon us.

We love because he first loved us (1 John 4:19).

Section Two defines the Transformation of the Heart healing paradigm, and also includes two healing stories and the "Healing Hands" prayer ministry. It details the Transformation of the Heart healing paradigm—the three human missions of transformation. All three missions relate to finding the truth of our heart (sifting through the many disguises), seeking forgiveness, and knowing that the mystery of God's love through the sacraments is vital to our wellbeing. The Lord knows infinitely more about our heart than we do. The receipt of the Sacramental Eucharist is our most powerful route to transformation in Christ's love, yet in the Transformation of the Heart journey, we enter into communion with God's love in prayer and receive healing grace as well. The Transformation of the Heart

Paradigm is rooted in the Great Commandment to love the Lord....

> *I give you a new commandment, that you love one another. Just as I have loved you, you also should love one another* (Mark 12:30).
> *and just as I have loved you, you also should love one another* (John 13:34).

The three interrelated missions of Transformation of the Heart are:

1. **Love-seeking mission.** *In our desire to love Jesus, we remember how to receive both God's love and human love, and we find where it has been lost. Lost love is where many needs for forgiveness lie. We find the enormity of God's love and come to know the intimacy of the Lord's desire to love us. Our heart awakens to love and we embrace our longing to love and to be loved.*

2. **Love-sharing mission.** *As we proceed in healing, we witness our capacity to increase the gift of love in us, to desire to love God and to love one another—especially those whom we have harmed or who have harmed us; and we learn to surrender into this desire to love, for the sake of truth and forgiveness in ourselves and in others.*

3. **Truth-seeking mission.** *As we learn to love and to be loved, the Lord shows us the emotional truth of our heart—made possible by the Lord's Resurrection and the presence of the Holy Spirit in each one of us. We are gifted with the enormity of God's love and compassion, and we are led to the truth of our needs for forgiveness, one small step at a time. We are led to our own truth and to our need to let go of the debris of sin. In the truth-seeking mission, we come to understand God's mission in us is for the sake of the Kingdom of Heaven—for the healing of the One Body of Christ.*

> *If you love me, you will keep my commandments. And I will ask the Father, and he will give you another Advocate, to be with you forever. This is the Spirit of truth, whom the world cannot receive, because it neither sees him nor knows him. You know him, because he abides with you, and he will be in you. I will not leave you orphaned; I am coming to you. Do not let your hearts be troubled, and do not let them be afraid* (John 14:15-18, 26-27).

It is through the human experience of these interconnected missions, united with the mission of the Lord—to bring each heart and soul to eternal justice through the sacrifice of his life—where we find glimpses of the purity of our heart. We come to know the Lord's profound desire to love all of humanity and for all to unite as one with Christ. The Sacred Heart of Christ represents justice for all, and is the source of love and consolation for all suffering and all truth.

Section Three includes glimpses into the Kingdom of Heaven—the eternal fulfillment of God's holy love. It also describes what is gained and what is lost in a healing journey with the Lord.

As we witness Jesus' love in the interior life of prayer, the Lord leads us to the truth of his eternal presence in us, where life and death are really one. As we uncover disguises of our heart and heal from our needs for forgiveness in ourselves and in others, deceit is replaced with the presence of love—in our heart and in our soul. Our entire being is illuminated with love, and we are led toward the fulfillment of the Lord's vision of our life purpose. Perhaps we are never fully prepared for the eternal presence of the Lord until the moment of our death, yet we are called toward the transformation of our heart and toward purity of heart that is free from deceit if not absolutely free from sin. We find that we can experience peace and joy in knowing that our heart and soul are filled with love, that we are fulfilling the Great Commandment to love. The fulfillment of love also designates our readiness to serve God with the fullness of love in our heart. We find the Kingdom of Heaven grace is present in us now, and we await with confidence the mystery of the eternal Kingdom.

The Lord leads us to grace so that our desire to love him can be fulfilled—by showing us his truth in our heart, helping us to forgive and to surrender in his love. Jesus already loves each one of us, yet it is our work to open our heart prayerfully to love and to be loved by the Lord so that we may find the disguise in our heart that clouds our seeing of our perfect love for the Lord. As our sin is healed, our love for the Lord increases. The payoff for healing sin is love and peace in our heart—and eternal life in God's love.

In my own longing to love the Lord, I am drawn to the heart of Christ where I witness the unfolding of my heart's truth of sins and my own remorse and sense of anguish. The heart that is filled with sin is sluggish. Yet with healing, the body, mind, spirit, and soul are renewed and refreshed, and the heart and spirit are set free to love and to be loved.

This book is not so much my personal revelation, as it is wisdom I have learned that may help lead others to their own personal revelation with the Lord and subsequent transformation of the heart—a transformation that leads to knowledge of one's true self, clarity of one's life purpose, and preparation for eternal life. This book includes both wisdom of God's love and blessings in God's love that I have received in my prayer practice.

Only Jesus can help us uncover the disguise that blocks our heart's way to our journey home, and only in grace can our heart truly be healed. This is the framework of the Transformation of the Heart journey. As we witness our deepest desire to be one with Christ, we open to our heart's fullness of truth as seen by the Lord—where we desire to hide nothing—for the sake of our own healing and for the healing of the One Body of Christ. In grace we are shown the truth so that we may be drawn to the fulfillment of love. All of this healing happens in the arms of Christ, truly preparing us to participate more fully in the sacraments of Reconciliation and the Eucharist, and in the liturgy of the Mass. To grasp the beauty of Jesus' love is indescribable, and this love is not just for a few, it is for all.

Pope John Paul II led the world toward love—through his own presence of love touching millions of people worldwide, through his daily practice of contemplative prayer, through his call to declare the year of the Eucharist in 2004–2005, and in his request that veneration of the Sacred Heart of Christ be faithfully restored:

> *For it is in the Heart of Christ that the human heart learns to know the true and unique meaning of its life and destiny; it is in the Heart of Christ that the human heart receives its capacity to love.*[1]

---

[1] Letter of John Paul II on the Sacred Heart on the occasion of the third centenary of the death of St. Margaret Mary, June 22, 1990, The Vatican.

In Pope John Paul II's visit to Paray-le-Monial in 1986, he spoke these words:

> In the Heart of Christ, one's heart learns to know the genuine and unique meaning of one's life and destiny, to understand the value of an authentically Christian life, to keep oneself from certain perversions of the human heart, and to unite the filial love of God and the love of neighbor. The true reparation asked by the Heart of the Savior will come when the civilization of the Heart of Christ can be built upon the ruins heaped up by hatred and violence. . . . For this reason, I desire that you pursue with persevering action, the spread of the genuine cult of the Heart of Christ.[2]

He also called the world to return to the mystical tradition—that all are called to union of love with Christ. In his apostolic letter at the close of the Jubilee Year in 2001, he wrote:

> This great mystical tradition . . . shows how prayer can progress, as a genuine dialogue of love, to the point of rendering the person wholly possessed by the divine Beloved, vibrating at the Spirit's touch, resting filially within the Father's heart.[3]

The word of God that is present in each and every heart has guided the words in this book—as I unite my heart with the Lord in a daily prayer practice of Lectio Divina. The primary call for me as I understand it is to express the Lord's desire for all people to open their heart to receive his love in all of its fullness—so that we can more fully love and be loved. I have written what has been captured through my heart as I have been both blessed and challenged with facing the truth of my own forgiveness needs, and in this, being shown how healing of the heart affects the healing of the body, mind, spirit, and soul.

When we allow the Lord to lead us, the word of the Lord draws us to our heart's desires, resulting in the transformation of our heart. As you read, you may remember what your soul has known since

---

[2] John Paul II, *Apostleship of Prayer and Devotion to the Sacred Heart*, from the Holy Father's visit to Paray-le-Monial, October 1986.

[3] John Paul II, Apostolic Letter at the Close of the Jubilee Year, *Novo Millennio In-etunte*, January 6, 2001.

its conception: The holy and compassionate love of the Lord Jesus Christ is given out to each and every soul conceived, and though it may be temporarily hidden from view, this love is abiding, steadfast, and eternal. This book includes knowledge that I have gleaned from prayer over many years. My hope is that the writings in this book further lead you to peace and to the beauty of the Word of God in you, and to joy from locating your own heart's desire to love and to serve in the fullness of God's love. In reading this book, you will see that locating the true self is possible through reflections of love that draw your heart toward Christ.

I am grateful to the Lord for the gift of life and the gift of knowing Jesus' love and presence in me for the sake of others. Through the paradigm of Transformation of the Heart made known by the Lord through my heart in prayer, my own heart has been raised and transformed on many occasions. I am healed in numerous ways and drawn to oneness with God's love for the sake of others and shown the Kingdom of Heaven grace. For this work and healing I am eternally grateful; I trust in God's goodness, not my own worthiness or capacities. The desire and longing in me to love Jesus has been partially fulfilled and met by Jesus' love in me. Although much deceit in my heart is lifted, sin is always before all of us, and I seek forgiveness from the Lord in each and every prayer. I know the greatness of the love of the Lord, and I know the freedom in my Spirit to unite with the heart of Christ for the sake of others and to pray for the One Body of Christ, the Church. My heart is filled with gratitude for all of these things. As you read the pages in this book, may you be blessed with all of Jesus' love in you and enlightened to your heart's needs as only the Lord can see them. That is God's gift to you.

A Soulful Attraction to Jesus

Sifting through inner thoughts no longer important
Mounting desire climbs to higher ecstasies
Nurturing love scales beyond comprehension
Drawn inward is the soul's reaching to God
Not to drown in sin
Eternally bequeathing in God's holy love.

Definitions

*Be kind to one another, tender-hearted, forgiving each other,
just as God in Christ also has forgiven you.
Therefore be imitators of God, as beloved children;
and walk in love, just as Christ also loved you and gave Himself up for us, an
offering and a sacrifice to God as a fragrant aroma*
(Eph 4:32–5:3).

A few definitions of language that I use often in the text might be helpful to the reader.

Humans, Sin, and the Debris of Sin

As humans, we are not perfect. Each one of us makes mistakes that harm others, and others make mistakes that do harm to us. These mistakes often involve sin, and with each sin or mistake made, we need to seek forgiveness.

Our own mistakes and the harm done to us by others produce in us—in varying degrees—emotions of guilt, shame, hurt, anger, and denial. These emotions are at the root of "the debris of sin." The debris of sin is the energetic form of sin that is held in the heart, spirit, soul, and physical body and interrupts the good health of the mind and physical body. When the heart is filled with love—when we are in union with God's love in prayer and in receipt of the Sacraments of the Church—our heart is healed. With each small healing, our soul is filled with God's love and light. As the soul's light dispels the darkness of sin, our health improves. This does not explain all illness by any means, but it is part of the mystery of the human condition and the healing that is possible in God's love. We seek God's love and healing from all sin, and we seek God's will in our recovery from illnesses of the body and the mind.

Kingdom of Heaven Grace

I use the words "Kingdom of Heaven grace" to describe the perfect love that exists in heaven, where all has been made perfect. It is my understanding that we can experience this grace now, and that in this grace, healing happens. We open to God's will in this grace as we pray, as we worship, and as we receive Sacraments of the Church. Believing in the presence of this grace at all times allows us to heal. In this grace, we can witness God's love, and our own love for all people, even those who have harmed us. As we are forgiven by the Lord, we also must forgive others, and love others—even those who have done us harm. In our faith, we trust in this love and grace to guide us in our prayers for forgiveness.

Gifts of the Holy Spirit

The Gifts of the Holy Spirit are made explicit in many scriptures. As our love for the Lord deepens (one way for this to happen is to engage in a daily practice of prayer and worship, contemplative or otherwise), and as is God's will in each person, we may receive over time a deeper experience and knowledge of the gifts of the Holy Spirit within.

St. Thomas Aquinas emphasizes that throughout scripture there are two groups of blessings that the Holy Spirit gives to those who receive him.

The twelve "Fruits of the Holy Spirit" that St. Paul names for us in his letter to the Galatians: love, joy, peace, patience, kindness, goodness, generosity, gentleness, faithfulness, modesty, self-control, and chastity (Galatians: 22-23). In addition, the Spirit endows us with blessings of the seven "Gifts of the Holy Spirit" that are intended to enable the soul with its natural good habits and power that help us to be responsive to the guidance and inspirations of God. The Gifts of the Holy Spirit appear when we are living in true, divine charity. When we love God above all things, and when we love all things for his sake, then that same spiritual fire of love makes us keenly sensitive to his direction. Thus the Gifts appear with charity, and in turn they lead back to greater holiness and to greater love. The prophet Isaiah speaks of these seven Gifts when he writes, prophesying about the coming of Christ:

> *A branch will sprout from the root of Jesse,*
> *and from his root a flower will rise up,*
> *and the spirit of the Lord will rest upon him:*
> *a spirit of wisdom and of understanding,*
> *a spirit of counsel and of fortitude,*
> *a spirit of knowledge and of piety, and he shall be*
> *filled with the spirit of the fear of the Lord*[1] (Isa 11:1-3).

I have frequently written in this book "knowing God's love and word in my heart." This means that the gifts of the Holy Spirit that have been made manifest in me include wisdom and understanding of God's love—that is also described as "oneness with Christ" in prayer where I witness the Kingdom of Heaven grace. I know humility of spirit in this gift. I am grateful for Jesus' merciful love. Most of all, I am grateful that in my desire to love him, I am at home. As I witness the beauty of God's love, my soul is risen in greater beauty than I have ever known—as I witness God's glory in prayer. The gifts of the Holy Spirit are not only present while we are on earth, but for all time.

The practice of transformation of the heart contemplative prayer helps us along our way, as we progress in the healing of our heart and the understanding of the nature of the gifts of the Holy Spirit in us, and how we each are called to use our gifts to build up the One Body of Christ, the Church.

Thomas Merton reminds us that all gifts are from God, and that humility of spirit is the only way to receive and to practice the gifts of the Holy Spirit for the sake of the Kingdom.

---

[1] Fr. Peter John Cameron, *The Gifts of the Holy Spirit, According to St. Thomas Aquinas* (New York: Archdiocese of New York, 2002).

Contemplative experience, whatever it may be, is a pure gift of God, and it has to be a gift, for that is part of its very essence. Indeed, contemplation itself is not necessarily a sign of worthiness or sanctity at all. It is a sign of the goodness of God, and it enables us to believe more firmly in his goodness, to trust in him more, above all to be more faithful in our friendship with him. Do not be surprised if contemplation springs out of pure emptiness, in poverty, dereliction, and spiritual night.[2]

One Body of Christ

The Bible is filled with scripture that teaches us about the One Body of Christ. First Corinthians, Chapter 12, relates the gifts of the Holy Spirit to the connectedness of all humanity. We are created in the image of God before birth, each one with a gift of the Holy Spirit, each one with the presence of Christ as love dwelling within. When one person is loved—we are all loved. When one person is left out or rejected, we are all left out and rejected. In the Liturgy of the Mass, the bread and wine are consecrated and become the real presence of the One Body of Christ. With each Eucharist received, God's blessing goes out to all people in all corners of the world.

The One Body of Christ is the Church—not a building or a denomination, but every human being that God created and the earth he made: everything that Jesus redeemed with his blood. We are all united, and we are all needed. When I pray with someone for healing, I pray not only for their specific healing needs, but also for the healing of the One Body of Christ, for the healing of humanity and the earth itself—all that God created and loves. As one is healed, the others are healed, too.

Belief in the One Body of Christ leads us to love and accept rather than judge and criticize one another. Part of loving our neighbor is accepting that all personality temperaments are God's design and that all gifts are needed. As we honor the Great Commandment, to love God with all that we are, we cannot separate our love for Christ from our love for all people. Holding this intention is one of our greatest calls. To heed the meaning of the One Body of Christ is to reject no one and to love all as we love God.

---

[2] Thomas Merton, *New Seeds of Contemplation* (New York: New Directions Publishing, 1961).

*For just as the body is one and has many members,
and all the members of the body, though many,
are one body, so it is with Christ.
As it is, there are many members, yet one body*
(1 Cor 12:13, 12:20).

*He himself is before all things, and in him all things hold together.
He is the head of the body, the church; he is the beginning,
the firstborn from the dead, so that he might come to have first
place in everything.
For in him all the fullness of God was pleased to dwell,
and through him God was pleased to reconcile to himself all
things, whether on earth or in heaven,
by making peace through the blood of the cross* (Col 1:18-20).

Section One

The Desire to Love Jesus

Overview

For this is how God loved the world: he gave his only Son, so that everyone who believes in him may not perish but may have eternal life (John 3:16).

I love Jesus. I have given my heart away to the Lord; the message of this book is what happens when one loves the Lord.

Just when I thought I had everything, I was faced with the possibility of losing my life to cancer. I responded by opening my heart to seek Jesus' assistance and this is when I first truly witnessed his love for me. If I had never opened my heart to Jesus' love, I would not be writing this book. I would not have experienced the personal healing or be enjoying the caring relationships I have today. A relationship with Christ leads to successful relationships with many others; it is the single most important relationship we have. In the depth of my heart, I know that God so loved the world, and so loves each soul. The Apostle John's scripture above awakens my heart to the deepest place of love I know. I believe both love and sorrow in this scripture, as Jesus died for my sins, too, and I love Jesus with all of my heart.

Personal remorse is more real when we acknowledge our love for the Lord and we believe the Lord loves each one of us.

Jesus' love is the source of all healing. As we open our hearts to love Jesus and allow Jesus' love to shine within us, we learn to trust God's mercy. It becomes the one thing we truly desire and need. "You show me your love for me, and I show you my love a thousand-fold." These are words of the Lord that I often know in my heart as I experience the generosity and goodness of Jesus' love.

Jesus' love is the source of all healing.

This book is about the nature of that love and how we might venture into prayer and discover our true self and our one true love, Jesus, by the opening of our heart to God's love, which is already present in our souls. The healing power of Jesus' love comes to us always from God the Father and Creator, and we participate in this grace in many ways—at Mass and through the Liturgy and the Sacraments, in prayer, in loving one another, and in loving the earth's resources. We prepare to receive the Lord by first opening our heart to receive love, and through Jesus' love to know the truth of our heart and our forgiveness needs. Through these reflections of truth with the Lord, we prepare for our fullest participation to love the Lord and to love one another. Through our knowing of truth in our heart, we may more fully prepare for Mass by receiving the Sacrament of Reconciliation.

God gifts us with the desire to love. In the intimacy of prayer, we understand the Trinity—God the Father, God the Son, and God the Holy Spirit—and we learn how to love each with distinction. Opening to God's love is a Trinitarian prayer. Loving God is the way to heal our hearts, deepen our faith, and understand the nature of the Trinity.

When we open our hearts to God's love, we also experience a sense of the "Kingdom of God" or heaven, a glimpse of eternity in our human condition on earth. We become intimately aware that as we are all one, life and death are also one.

God's love for humanity extends to all of Creation. We can never forget our reliance on and connection with one another, the earth, and all of nature. As we pray for one another, we also pray for the healing of the "One Body of Christ" and for all of Creation. Elements of the earth are also healing to the physical body and to the One Body of Christ.

Love for the Lord is beyond our knowing of all other love. Once our hearts awaken to an intimacy of love with Jesus in prayer, we are off and running with our daily prayer practice; we want to return and stay devoted to our love for Christ, which is most vivid to us in prayer and in giving our love to God. God gifts us once again by drawing our heart to him. In interior prayer, we find our heart's true desires—what we cannot find language for or even knowledge of through our minds. Our human heart is united with the heart of Christ, so we are gifted with divine love that leads us to truth, to self, and to our need for forgiveness.

The inward journey to divine love and to our own forgiveness needs is not for the weak or faint at heart, yet it is the Word of God that we praise at Mass that gives us the love and strength to pursue our own loneliness. The desire to love Jesus draws the heart to know and to heal the human condition of loneliness. It is sin, I believe, that creates the condition of loneliness, not only our own sins, but also the sins committed against us. Today, people may seek a soul mate when their heart is lonely from the condition of sin, and inadvertently many more sins are committed while they sort out finding the right person. Our first and eternal soul mate is the Lord, who desires to cleanse our heart from sin, and then our heart is free to locate and to love our human soul mate.

Over time, we come to trust in God's will and seek to surrender to it in our lives. Naturally, this takes time and occurs in small steps. All scripture begins to make sense, each daily reading applying directly to the day. We come to know Jesus Christ as Teacher, as Beloved, as God of all Creation, as Physician of our bodies and souls. We come to understand that each moment of grace is eternal and that there is hope through the Resurrection for our everlasting presence with Christ. We realize that we desire Jesus' eternal presence and communion more than anything.

Through the interior experience of desire for communion with the Lord, we come to know the desire to receive the Holy Eucharist in the Liturgy, the body and blood of Christ. As Jesus offers us his love, we know this is the most intimate expression of his desire to love us.

This section includes four chapters:

Chapter One: An Embrace with God

Chapter Two: The Greatest Commandment

Chapter Three: Drawn to a Divine Proclamation

Chapter Four: "Little Spirit of Jesus"

As you read, consider these questions:

What does it mean to open your heart to receive Jesus' love for you? In opening your heart to love the Lord, in what way does Jesus draw you to the desire to love him?

Chapter One

An Embrace with God

*My one desire and my one joy should be to know:
Here is the thing that God has willed for me.
In this his love is found, and in accepting this
I can give back his love to him and give myself with it to him.
For in giving myself I shall find him and he is life everlasting.*[1]

I almost waited too long. I remember how my mother used to tell everyone about my independent streak. I would never accept help from anyone, I had to do it all myself. I raised myself, I put myself through college, I was too independent to get married, etc., etc. She was proud of me for that, so I was proud of myself. Yet I remember her relief when I introduced her to the man I was going to marry (at age 38). "Finally," she said, "someone to take care of you."

Self-determination can be overdone, especially in early childhood. As for me, without knowing it, I closed my heart to receiving love. I assumed I was loved, but I didn't open my heart to receive it. Opening your heart to receive love and to give love is not something to be taken for granted—especially when it comes to God's love. We search for grace, and sometimes, just because we need it, grace finds us.

---

1 Thomas Merton, *New Seeds of Contemplation* (New York: New Directions Publishing, 1961).

When I received a diagnosis of breast cancer at age 40, I feared that I had waited too long to ask for help. I turned to God—and even that didn't come easily for me. I awoke in the middle of the night in May 1994, and sat up in bed with my fingers curled around a lump. This was more than an awakening from sleep. I knew God was alerting me to breast cancer. That was a timely miracle. It occurred one week before the birth of our second child, Izak. Bria was 2½ years old. I called my family doctor who told me not to worry, it was probably a clogged milk duct and I could wait until after I gave birth to be tested. I told him I felt I needed to act on it now. I knew God's presence in the night was probably not announcing a clogged milk duct.

I gave birth and was diagnosed with breast cancer a few days later. This was followed by several biopsies, with the news getting worse with each one. After breastfeeding for a few weeks, I learned that I needed a mastectomy. I was afraid I might die. It was terrifying to love two small children so much and to be fully aware that I might not survive to raise them.

Outdoors, on the path to our family sweathouse, I made a deal with God. I knelt down, felt the dirt in my hands, and with tears falling, I asked God if I could please live to raise my children. In return, I promised, I would do anything he wanted. I didn't get a clear answer in those moments, although I did experience God's consoling love and, looking back, I would say that my fears of death subsided some.

That same day I received a St. Therese of Lisieux prayer card in the mail from Aunt Tootsie, my 90-year-old "cowgirl" aunt who lived in Bend, Oregon; she had been receiving treatments for brain cancer. I admired her for her beauty, her strength, and her faith. She wrote on her battered card that she prayed each day. Like my dad, Aunt Tootsie never missed a Sunday Mass. I gripped her card tightly each day as I prayed. She also wrote that God could not possibly be taking me away when I had two beautiful children to raise. I took some solace in the thought and made a choice to believe her.

My surgeon soon called to discuss the mastectomy. Before I even knew I had breast cancer, he had come to my birthing room simply to introduce himself. He told me his wife had given birth a few weeks earlier in the same room. His story and his brief appearance comforted me—I sensed his compassion and his confidence that I would be all right. Prayer is healing, and shared story—even a brief one in medical settings—can also draw one's heart to a sense of the familiar, and hope for wellness.

He explained that following the mastectomy, they could determine if they had "got it all." Those words were frightening—to have to undergo a procedure to remove my huge breast filled with milk, and then to still be afraid of the disease. I could not imagine how they could remove my breast. It was incomprehensible, yet the larger question of cancer loomed over me. There was no such thing as being "prepared" for this surgery. I was afraid. I remember being wheeled away to the operating room, leaving my husband and my friend, Joyce—I have never felt so alone.

The story goes that as you pray to St. Therese, she will bring you a rose to let you know of her intercession. As I awoke in the recovery room after the removal of my breast, the first thing my blurry eyes saw was a brilliant red rose of St. Therese on the bed stand next to me. The rose bush was a gift from colleagues at the University of Washington; they were nearly strangers to me yet they sent this beautiful rose bush. In a moment of grace, I knew God's words in my heart: "Pray fervently each day and I will behold you in all your suffering."

"Pray fervently each day and I will behold you in all your suffering."

That was 17 years ago, and I don't believe I'll quit praying anytime soon. I am grateful to them and to St. Therese. The rose bush is planted at the entrance to our outdoor swimming pool in the woods, and still produces large, deep red roses.

In moments of profound grace, my spirit was ignited with the desire to love God and serve God. I had no idea at the time just how much healing I was in for, or that I would come to know the suffering of Jesus and of others as well. God saved my life from the disease of breast cancer and saved my children from the loss of their mother.

God has also kept his promise to behold me in my suffering from sin and the debris of sin. I have come to understand "the debris of sin" as the release of the energy of sin held in my physical body, thereby restoring my health and contributing to the healing of the One Body of Christ. My gratitude to God, and desire to love God, increases daily.

I was dreading the potentially fateful phone call from my surgeon, who was to report on the lab results and tell me whether I still had cancer. If I did, I knew I was facing a punishing regimen of chemotherapy and/or radiation. I went to bed and crawled under my covers. My mother and sister were in the house taking care of the kids, and my husband Bruce went to the office. The surgeon called the house, and my sister told him I was asleep, so he called Bruce and told him I was "cancer free." Bruce called my sister, who drew with huge magic markers three white posters announcing my renewed health and hung them on the fireplace. When I came downstairs from my nap I read the posters. I thought my sister and mother were just being optimistic, so I smiled and walked past them to get a cup of coffee. When I realized it was true that my cancer was gone, I laughed and cried at the same time. We all did. I prayed daily to St. Therese for many months.

In this story, I had to open my heart to God's love. Sometimes life bumps us into new territory where our usual resistance to God is thrust aside. I was afraid not to turn to God.

From the moment I was diagnosed with cancer, my heart was gripped with fear. Even with Jesus at my side, the fear did not leave me for a moment until I learned that the cancer was gone. Many people must live with fear because the disease is not cured before their death. Since my experience of breast cancer, I have learned to "hand over to Jesus" my fears and inescapable traumas. As I witness Jesus holding my trauma, I am able to receive and experience his infinite goodness and healing love. This is vital because it is difficult to participate in our own healing when the heart is locked in fear. My life and comforts of life matter, but his love is first.

I had many, smaller wake-up calls from God before this one—yet with each one I would do an approach-avoidance dance with God. I sensed that I had great needs, and I knew I was drawn to Spirit, yet it took a long time for me to truly respond with my heart to God's drawing me to him. Today, I would say that God saving my life was huge, yet it pales beside the healing of my heart from sin, which I firmly believe has also healed me at a cellular level. It is in the goodness of God's healing grace that I am able to deepen my love for Jesus and my desire for healing of the One Body of Christ.

Even before the breast cancer, I knew that "Spirit" was alive in me for some purpose. But I misunderstood—I thought it meant that I was to become a "healer." Today, I understand that Jesus is the healer and God is asking me to pray for others and to help others to turn inward to the Lord and to understand the healing properties of God's love that dwells within. In Jesus' goodness, His love is ever present and fulfilled in each one of us through the Resurrection for our life, our breath, our joys—and our healing.

Chapter Two

The Greatest Commandment

> *You shall love the Lord your God with all your heart,*
> *and with all your soul, and with all your mind.*
> *This is the greatest and first commandment.*
> *And a second is like it: You shall love your neighbor as yourself.*
> *On these two commandments hang all the law and the prophets*
> (Matt 22:37-40).

When Jesus spoke these words, he gave humanity the key that opens the secret door to healing, and the discovery of the meaning of life and the heart's abundant capacity to love. As we love with all of our heart, soul, understanding, and strength, Jesus heals us in our heart, soul, understanding, and strength. We come to know this love with Jesus, most of all in the Sacrament of the Eucharist, but also in the interior life of prayer. This experience of grace, as we fully love Jesus, is difficult to put into words, yet our healing lies in believing that any hope for peace in our hearts, and in the world, is found in the promise of this commandment.

This commandment is tied to my devotion to the Sacred Heart of Jesus. Someone gave me a prayer card, and I said the daily prayer for months. One day at Mount Angel Abbey and Seminary in Oregon, I was praying before a statue of the Sacred Heart and the Lord showed me the truth of my heart, which at the time was deep sorrow. My mother had been diagnosed with lung cancer, and in order to cope with the serious news, I was on an overnight spiritual retreat at the Abbey. I stayed in front of the statue until my tears subsided, and Jesus consoled and loved me. My own heart was drawn to love Jesus and to seek healing for the One Body of Christ. I took a photograph of this statue and carry it today in my Bible.

The Sacred Heart of Jesus, for me, reflects more than anything his infinite love for us, and his desire for us to remember that his merciful love brings healing to all people. When we remember his love for us, we desire to love Jesus and are able to grow in our capacity to love him with all of our heart and our strength.

As I give my heart to Christ in prayer, I am aware of my devotion to the truth of my faith. The Holy Spirit, as Truth—given out to all through the Resurrection—is the centerpiece of my faith and my grounding, so to speak, in prayer. I experience the grace of the Holy Spirit as truth and as love. Jesus has my heart, and I desire understanding of the deep personal truth of his incarnation, life teachings, passion, death, resurrection, and ascension. I also desire the truth of my own forgiveness needs and I want to pray for the healing of the One Body of Christ. My heart engages in these mysteries of our faith, and all of this becomes part of my breath and my love. We are drawn to devotion and praise of the Lord through prayers to the Sacred Heart.

As we love Jesus, we are intimately aware of our own need for forgiveness, and we hold prayers for forgiveness of others. Each prayer is love for Jesus, devotion to Jesus, and a seeking of forgiveness.

St. Margaret Mary Alacoque, a French nun, initiated the official devotion to the Sacred Heart of Jesus in the 17th century, after the Lord appeared to her on several occasions. In one of these visions he showed her his heart, pierced with a wound, encircled with a crown of thorns, surrounded by flames, and surmounted by a cross—this image is shown worldwide today. The Lord commanded her to practice and to teach the devotion to his Sacred Heart, because of his ardent desire to be loved and his wish to give to all the treasures of his love and mercy. The Catholic Church considers worship of the Sacred Heart as supreme adoration because it is paid to the physical Heart of Christ, considered not only mere flesh, but as truly united to the Divinity.

On the third centenary of her death, Pope John Paul II issued a letter calling for the veneration to the Sacred Heart to be faithfully restored:

> *For it is in the Heart of Christ*
> *that the human heart learns to know the true and unique*
> *meaning of its life and destiny; it is in the Heart of Christ*
> *that the human heart receives its capacity to love.*[1]

As we come to understand the nature of love through the heart of Christ, we come to understand our true selves. Jesus shows himself to me through this devotion, teaching me how to love and how to be loved. As I have learned to love, I have found my truth and life purpose. Perhaps our desire to love Jesus and our desire to live out our life purpose are one and the same.

In contemplating the heart of Christ, we learn to receive God's love and beauty. We receive through the heart of Christ, the capacity to love him, and we want to open our heart to receive his love and guidance.

The heart of Christ, the Great Commandment, and the sacraments of the Eucharist and Reconciliation should never be separated from one another. In contemplative prayer, these mysteries unfold in us as we deepen our relationship with Jesus. Pope John Paul II further writes in his letter:

> *In Christ Jesus is fulfilled the fullness of the commandment of the Old Testament: "You shall love the Lord with all your heart"*
> *(Deut 6:5); in fact, only the Heart of Christ has loved the Father with an undivided love.*[2]

---

[1] Letter of John Paul II on the Sacred Heart on the occasion of the third centenary of the death of St. Margaret Mary, June 22, 1990, The Vatican.

[2] Ibid.

In the same letter, Pope John Paul II invites all to active participation in the Eucharist and the Sacrament of Penance, intimately bound to the humanity of Christ. He also calls us to meditate on the Word of God, in prayers of adoration of the Sacred Heart that place us "in the closest, most intimate relationship with his Heart that has so loved human beings."[3]

The second part of the Great Commandment is to love one another. As we deepen our capacity to love Jesus and become aware that our heart is united with Christ's heart, we may experience grace moving through us for the love of the "other." Jesus shows me this grace with great beauty, yet each and every person can also experience this when they receive the Sacrament of the Eucharist and when they pray intentionally for all people. Our absolute love for Jesus is showered upon our "neighbor." Whether or not we know the person is insignificant; Jesus knows where grace is needed. In this depth of love, we surrender the fullness of ourselves without intention, other than that the will of God and the grace of the Holy Spirit go out to the world. We see Christ in the "other" and we love this person as we love Jesus. The words that I know at this place of the prayer are "The Kiss of the Holy Spirit is upon you," and the "other" receives God's blessing; I know God's blessing of myself as well in each prayer.

The freedom to love is the heart's expression of the healing of the soul. The Holy Spirit is present in each one of us for this holy purpose. "My love is without measure" and "My love is all-healing" are Jesus' words that my heart knows well, in union with his love.

The commandment to love draws my heart to the deepest love that I know. When I pray, my heart is centered in love for Jesus and Jesus draws me closer. I simply rest with my heart's knowing of grace in Jesus' love. In the Lord's goodness, I surrender in prayer and let go, asking for God's will to be served for the sake of others.

Everything in this book rests on this Great Commandment, and on the gift of the Holy Spirit as love poured out to each of us at Pentecost—allowing us to know the desire to love Jesus and to love all. As we learn to love Jesus and to pray, we bring healing to our family, friends, community, and world.

---

[3] Ibid.

Chapter Three

Drawn to a Divine Proclamation

So, Jesus, there is no need to say:
In drawing me, draw also the souls I love.
The simple words "Draw me" are enough!
When a soul has been captivated by the intoxicating odor
of Your ointments,
she cannot run alone.
Every soul she loves is drawn after her—
a natural consequence of her being drawn to you.[1]
St. Therese of Lisieux

Jesus draws our hearts to the desire to love him. There is no greater gift—as this is divine union with the Lord and we know the healing presence of grace. The gift of "desire to love Jesus" is made manifest in the gift of the Holy Spirit, which is Jesus' love for each one of us. We turn to the Holy Spirit in us, then, to receive the gift of the desire to love—and of this internal yearning or longing, we are most likely familiar, even if we have not yet defined the source or meaning of longing. Longing is simply our desire to love the Lord, as this gift is given out to the world and resides in our spirit

---

1 John Beevers, Translator, *The Autobiography of St. Therese of Lisieux: The Story of a Soul* (New York: Image Books/Doubleday, 2001).

and soul. This is hardly a great challenge—to have Jesus' love—the challenge is perhaps in our capacity to surrender our own will long enough for Jesus to draw us closer. This requires that we put our self-interests aside long enough to seek and trust Jesus' interests and will in us—and this is all about the desire to love and to be loved.

What follows is a story of how Jesus appeared to me in grace, showing me the desire to love.

My heart and desire to love Jesus were drawn in an extraordinary way in the days before the death of Pope John Paul II. Our family kept a candle lit on our dining table during the last few days of the Pope's life—both as a reminder that a holy person was dying and as a call to pray for him, his family, his community, and the world. Upon his death, the Lord touched my heart with grace, calling me to pray for him. I surrendered deeply in prayer to Jesus and sensed God the Father's presence. I truly felt the Pope's presence as a Saint praying for me and for the world. I felt the Pope's presence, with a huge smile, saying: "That should be enough." I believe he was referring to grace flooding my entire being. In God's grace, I felt the Pope's spirit pass over me as if he was already pure love. I felt a great love for God and for the Pope. I was so grateful for his prayer for the world. I was moved into an ecstasy with God's love as the words in this prose came through me in an instant; I could hardly type fast enough to keep up. I felt the Lord inspiring words of wisdom to my heart—that the Pope's dying prayer was for everyone in the world to desire to love Jesus Christ. This experience happened by God's goodness alone; I said "yes" to God's will. This is that poem.

His Holiness in Flight—April 2, 2005

Unsurpassed heights
with no ceiling to God's love.
Surrender into the night
as galaxies await movement in your heart.
Behold a holy moment of truth
in a loved one's passing.

Pope John Paul II's demise
is the greatest surrender on Earth to God's will—
for each person to desire to love Jesus
with the fullness of their heart
is the Holy Father's passing prayer.

> *God who hears all prayers, all Masses said,*
> *stands arms outstretched*
> *greeting each word, each prayer, each host given.*
> *Hearts aglow with Resurrection love*
> *The Holy Father's prayer kindles love*
> *in global proportions—blessings to endure forever.*
>
> *Burning is your heart, opening to God's love*
> *Firmament—of earth well prepared for nourishment*
> *with global intentions*
> *is the Holy Father's passing*
> *in a star-filled grace.*
>
> *Like a missile*
> *is His Holiness in flight.*
> *Of love, of peace to all nations alike*
> *Not a hair disturbed in a moment of time*
> *in the passing of His Holiness.*
>
> *Pray once more*
> *for love to abound to all souls in God's Creation.*
> *Reply with resounding hope*
> *For peace and love in every heart alike.*
> *The gift of the season lies in hope*
> *for the Earth's transformation in love.*

Our home was filled with peace for days to come. I truly felt the Pope's spirit graced us with his love and prayers. Only in God's greatness could I know and experience this fire in my heart, where I felt a strong sense of love and peace for all others and nothing else held much importance.

Years later, it pleased me to read the Pope's reflection on the desire to love Jesus through the face of Christ. Asked what was the most important legacy of the Jubilee Year 2000, he said, "If we ask what is the core of the great legacy, it leaves us, but I would not hesitate to describe it as the contemplation of the face of Christ."[2]

The beauty of the face of Christ is captured as a central message in scripture as well:

---

[2] Patricia Treece, *Meet John XXIII: Joyful Pope and Father to All* (Cincinnati: Servant Books, St. Anthony Messenger Press, 2008).

> *And all of us, with unveiled faces, seeing the glory*
> *of the Lord as though reflected in a mirror,*
> *are being transformed into the same image*
> *from one degree of glory to another;*
> *for this comes from the Lord, the Spirit* (2 Cor 3:18).

I know this glance of Jesus' love through the face of Christ, and it is a most tender love beyond any human love. It is infinite mercy, compassion, and a drawing of my heart toward Jesus in a complete surrender to the will of God. Contemplating the face of Christ, I give up other thoughts and needs, as if I had none other than to love and to receive divine love. Grace flows with bounty; Jesus is in no hurry and gives me no conditions. My heart is open and filled with love.

Of all the ways Pope John Paul II led the world, perhaps his greatest gift was his prayer that all would desire to love Jesus Christ, so that each and every soul would know healing and the grace of the Kingdom of Heaven.

Part of our humility as we experience the desire to love Jesus is to know without a doubt that no one is rejected from Jesus' love. Another Pope, Pope John Paul XXIII, had a crucifix hanging above his bed where he died. These words were written next to the crucifix: "The secret of my life—He died for everyone; no one is rejected from his love, from his forgiveness."[3] It took time for me to believe that I was included in Jesus' love—maybe my sins or the sins against me were too great. This is why we need the gift of the "desire to love Jesus." When we are in the presence of Christ with the desire to love him, nothing else matters and we believe that we, too, are loved.

> *When we are in the presence of Christ with the desire to love him, nothing else matters and we believe that we, too, are loved.*

---

3 Archimandrite Sophrony, *Wisdom From Mount Athos: The Writings of Staretz Ilouan* (Mowbrays, London/Oxford, 1974; Alden Press, Osney Mead, Oxford).

*The Holy Spirit is love;
and the souls of all the holy
who dwell in heaven overflow with this love.
And on earth this same Holy Spirit
is in the souls of those who love God.*[4]

---

[4] Ibid.

Chapter Four

"Little Spirit of Jesus"

The psalmist's words, "My soul thirsts for God, for the living God. When shall I come and behold the face of God?" (Ps 42:2), were especially touching to Thomas Aquinas. He knew that in all of our desires, whether we realize it or not, we are really thirsting for God. Our every desire is an ache to enjoy and to be content with God's infinite sweetness.[1]

In the interior of prayer, I often know the tender love of Jesus, and at times I sense in my heart he calls me by a spiritual name. The name that most deeply moves my heart is "Little Spirit of Jesus." It was first given to me in my heart's knowing by the Lord one evening as I was falling asleep. Here is the story.

I was trying to get to sleep after working on a paper on Medieval Mysticism for a graduate course at Seattle University's School of Theology and Ministry. Each time I began to doze, I found myself at a place of sweet union with Jesus, and I heard myself whisper: "I love you, Jesus." My heart was being drawn to the Lord Jesus, and I could say or do nothing else. I knew a profound sense of beauty, love, and desire to love Jesus—I experienced

---

1 Mary Ann Fatula, *Thomas Aquinas: Preacher and Friend*, Way of the Christian Mystics series (Collegeville, MN: Liturgical Press, 1993).

divine tenderness in my heart. I could feel the Spirit of Jesus in my heart, over my heart, through my heart, and beneath my heart.

In these moments, I knew that Jesus' presence and his tender love for me were eternal. I knew the oneness in this grace—that life and death are one and that the grace of the Kingdom of Heaven is available to everyone now, yet made perfect in the Kingdom upon our death. Knowing that the lines between death and ever after life were blurred, I rested in this glorious love, professing my own quiet love for Jesus, knowing that my desire to love the Lord is also ever after. The night was filled with a quiet beauty and peace in my heart.

In the morning, I knew the words of the Lord: "Be my little spirit of Jesus, and bring souls to me. Justice is upon you."

Being completely surrendered to the heart of Christ, I responded simply, "Yes, Lord Jesus Christ." I was pleased with the name I had been given, and I felt blessed with the anticipation of eternal life. I am certain this experience of divine love and naming by the Lord is not for me alone, but comes in a special way to each person. I did nothing to earn this; it was all in Jesus' goodness and love for all of humanity that I was shown his tender love.

The Lord's peace stayed in my heart for two more days. I felt I had all of Jesus' love, yet I knew "all" of Jesus' love is for each person—somehow I felt I held all of it and it was perfect!

Many over the ages have written about such desire to love Jesus as I witnessed and have described. Open your heart to God's love, and God is there.

Jesus' Words On My Breath

Blessings of love received
With an infinite tenderness
Of a father
Of a mother
Showered upon me
In the stillness of the morning dew
Before daylight is lit
With the words of Jesus on my breath
Drawing my love deeper yet, for my heart to open
Tears befall me
In sight is only tenderness
My Beloved calls my name

> *Little spirit of Jesus*
> *His heart touches my own . . .*
> *a foreshadow of the Kingdom's light and love.*

In these moments of grace with the Lord, I allowed Jesus to hold my heart and I knew he was well pleased with my love. The desire to love Jesus is the meaning of human existence.

I trust that Jesus drew my heart to this tenderness of love also to teach me that this tenderness of love is possible on earth. To love one another with such tenderness is also possible at one's death, if we are sensitive to the nature of the human condition upon death. Today, as I provide care to those who are dying and to family members and friends gathered, I am reminded by the Lord of his infinite tenderness and love that are ever present. Recently, upon a person's last breath, the words "Praise be to God" and "God is good" came quietly and softly through my own breath, as the person drew his last breath. The Lord's tenderness of love and touch appeared to be present in some fashion or another in each person in the room—either in their voice or their touch, and in the slowness of tears flowing down their faces. I often sense that love is gained at the time of death—a person is lost, but love is not lost—a new kind of love is gained with the eternal presence of Christ, and hope for our eternal rest with one another.

The desire to love Jesus is the meaning of human existence.

Section Two

Healing Ministries of God's Love

Overview

The quest for purity of heart is necessary to a right prayer.
The possession of purity of heart is necessary to perfect prayer.[1]
John Cassian, 4th century monk

We may seek purity of heart—to live in the fullness of Christ, and to pray in perfect union with God's love—or perhaps we feel this is for a select few. It is for everyone, but it requires our participation. This section is about the heart's transformation into Christ's love—beginning with the desire to love the Lord and consenting to a journey of healing our heart—until we reach a glimpse of the fullness of God's love that is purity of heart.

A new heart I will give you, and a new spirit I will put within you; and I will remove from your body the heart of stone and give you a heart of flesh. I will put my spirit within you, and make you follow my statutes and be careful to observe my ordinances (Ezek 36:26).

---

[1] Colm Luibheid, Translation and Preface, *John Cassian Conferences* (New York: Paulist Press, 1985).

This section includes four chapters. Each chapter illustrates ways that God's love transforms the heart and shows how the heart's healing affects the body, mind, spirit, and soul. In these chapters we see how our love for the Lord is made manifest in us, and the Lord's response to our love is grace and healing, with a deepening of our trust that Jesus' love is for us and in us.

This section includes four chapters:

Chapter Five: Transformation of the Heart Healing Paradigm

Chapter Six: How to Begin

Chapter Seven: Two Personal Healing Stories

Chapter Eight: Healing Hands Prayer

The spiritual journey with Christ is one of transformation. As Jesus transforms the water into wine at the wedding feast of Cana, so he himself is transformed into the bread and wine in each Eucharistic sacrifice. This is for one purpose: his desire for the transformation of our heart and soul in the Body and Blood of Christ so that we may be fulfilled on earth as we will be in the Kingdom of Heaven.

The Transformation of the Heart healing paradigm is a journey of the heart and conversion from sin. Most importantly, it awakens a deepening in our knowing the presence of the love of the Lord in us. This healing paradigm involves three interconnected missions: the Truth-Seeking Mission, the Love-Seeking Mission, and the Love-Sharing Mission. The heart's healing also draws us to a keener awareness of God's love in the Liturgy of the Mass and sacraments, and in the interior practice of our prayer where we reflect on Jesus' love in the Gospel and the condition of our own heart.

While Jesus is our best teacher of prayer, there is a brief chapter here laying out how to get started in prayer, applying principles of Transformation of the Heart.

The Healing Hands prayer ministry described in Chapter 8 is rooted in Scripture, and is an extension of Transformation of the Heart. This section includes specific prayers for the person receiving healing and for those laying hands on, and a protocol for the healing prayer.

All of these are rooted in opening the heart to the Triune God's desire to love and to heal us. As you read these chapters and prayers, may your heart be opened to the fullness of God's grace. As Paul wrote in Trinitarian thought and language,

> *The grace of the Lord Jesus Christ, the love of God,*
> *and the communion of the Holy Spirit be with all of you*
> (2 Cor 13:13).

When we take these words to heart, we know and trust that we, too, are loved by the Lord Jesus Christ, and there can be no greater love.

Chapter Five

Transformation of the Heart
Healing Paradigm

The Holy Spirit inspires truth in us—teaching and forming us into the truth whose spirit he is. Most intimately of all, the spirit gives us the light to understand and speak the wonderful truth about God. For this Spirit of the son who is truth itself teaches us through love what our minds alone could never know.[1]
    Thomas Aquinas

To understand who God is, is to understand oneself. Transformation of the Heart is experiencing God through love, growing in an intimate and sweet relationship—in love and through love. As we love Jesus with all our heart, we are drawn to a more expansive and infinite knowledge of him than words can describe. Yet in our desire and in the Lord's drawing us inward to this desire, we know that we are found by God and there is no better place to be. We want to give all that we are to God, yet all that God asks of us is to love him with all of our being, and to love and care for one another. This intimacy of love is given freely to us in the Transformation of the Heart journey, and there is no greater joy than to witness this love.

---

[1] Mary Ann Fatula, *Thomas Aquinas: Preacher and Friend* (Collegeville, MN: Liturgical Press, 1993).

In everything we ask for, we are seeking God, who is the only answer to our thirst for love, our desire to love that lies within. This inner place has no apparent voice, understanding, or even hearing—yet the mystery of desire is what draws us to the mysteries of Christ's love for us. Our heart desires to be one with Christ for the sake of the Kingdom—and everything that lies between our own creation of self and eternal life is in need of transformation within our heart. We cannot know this purity of desire without first knowing a glimpse of the purity of our heart—and that is the journey of Transformation of the Heart. Our soul looks to our heart and waits for love to replace the places of darkness. Purity of heart is Jesus' gift to us, yet the Lord waits for our participation. Why do we need to participate? Perhaps we feel we have already "arrived" with God, yet there is always more to do up until our death and the Lord desires and aches to draw us nearer, to have the fullness of our love for him.

Transformation of the Heart is primarily about seeking Jesus' wisdom and truth of what lies in our heart that needs healing—and as the heart heals, the body, mind, spirit, and soul are also healed. Jesus sees our heart more clearly than we do; we hold our own disguises tightly. This is the reason, I believe, that the Lord revealed to me, through the Holy Spirit, Transformation of the Heart as a healing paradigm—to heal my own heart and to be offered to others. The Lord led me through the healing of my own heart and into the heart of Christ, wherein all sin lies and where all healing is possible. Healing of the Heart involves not only conversion from our own sins, but also healing from sin done to us by others, and the debris of sin held in the body.

Transformation of the Heart has direct roots in Lectio Divina, which goes back to the fourth and 5th centuries—the eager seeking after the Word of God as the way that God's truth is given to us. Traditionally, there are four Latin equivalents to express the four steps of Lectio: Lectio, Meditatio, Oratio, and Contemplatio—or reading (of scripture), meditation, prayer, and contemplation. It was brought to the West from the Eastern desert fathers by John Cassian at the beginning of the 5th century, and has been closely connected to St. Benedict and Benedictine spirituality. Lectio uses the senses in perceiving the works of the Lord; meditatio uses the intellect to reflect upon the insights presented in Lectio; oratio calls forth one's feelings to personalize new insights so that one may enter into a personal dialogue with the Lord, and contemplatio uses the intuition to coalesce the experience. In the quiet, one is open to the inspirations of the Holy Spirit which may come as new insights; new perceptions; new infusion of peace, joy, and love—all part of the mystical union of which the Saints tell us. One thing is for sure . . . we become intimate with the Lord in a regular Lectio Divina practice.

Transformation of the Heart is a form of Lectio and contemplative prayer that is centered on the heart. I gained insight into the paradigm over several years of doing healing prayer for others. The paradigm is simple, yet I have found a depth in healing in myself and in others that surpasses anything I could have expected. As I hold Transformation of the Heart retreats for others, I see participants receive healing in body, mind, spirit, and soul. The healing paradigm provides a structure for a prayer practice that will enhance anyone's gifts and relationship with the Lord.

This chapter provides a detailed description of the three interconnected missions that make up the Transformation of the Heart healing paradigm: The Truth-Seeking Mission, the Love-Seeking Mission, and the Love-Sharing Mission. Chapter six gives more information about Transformation of the Heart as a form of contemplative prayer, with suggestions for getting started.

The Truth-Seeking Mission. The Truth-Seeking Mission requires our surrender into God's love for us. This mission captures the essence of what is possible in the divine union of love with Jesus. We begin to hear more clearly the Holy Spirit within our heart—the wisdom of our heart is shown to us, including our own needs for forgiveness and healing from others' sins against us. Seeking truth of what has lain in disguise in the heart is the central cause or need in healing.

Seeking truth of what has lain in disguise in the heart is the central cause or need in healing.

As Thomas Aquinas teaches us: "The Holy Spirit speaks to us in two voices; one voice is the preached word of Scripture which we hear with our ears, and the Spirit also speaks interiorly to our heart—that only believers hear his voice."[2] Only God can convert our hearts, and our invitation is to love God with all of our heart; then we may hear the second voice that is central to our healing and eternal life.

We witness small steps of truth as the presence of Christ prepares us for forgiveness of self and others. With our love in union with God's love, the Holy Spirit moves our heart to discern the next piece of truth that we are ready for. As we witness the truth of our heart's need for forgiveness, we surrender to the Lord the harm done to us or that we have done to others. We pray for the healing of the One Body of Christ—this is God's action as well as our participation in prayer and faith. We let go to God whatever binds our heart. Over time, as the edges of our heart soften, we begin to see more clearly God's true purpose in us. This mission, like all three, is a mission that we pursue during our entire lifetime. There is always more truth to find, and truth is always healing.

Transformation of the Heart healing is good preparation for the Sacraments of Reconciliation and the Eucharist. We begin to notice how the heart can lie in disguise of sin, and how the Lord is ever present for small steps toward healing. When we surrender into God's love, we also notice that we sometimes need courage in our faith to proceed in our own truth—yet, unwinding even the most challenging of sins is possible in God's loving arms. As we long for Jesus' love, we also long for the truth of our own heart. We recognize that our growing freedom to love is God's gift to us in our conversion.

The Love-Seeking Mission. The Love-Seeking Mission is the opening of our heart to the presence of Christ's love in us—by the power of the Resurrection and the sending out of the Spirit into each person. We open our heart to the great passion of God's love for us and for all, that is entirely present within. In our faith and in our prayer, we trust in the ever-expanding capacity of the heart to open and to grow in love. As we open our heart to receive Jesus' love for us, we are going beyond words—we are seeking the action of our

---

2 Mary Ann Fatula, *Thomas Aquinas: Preacher and Friend* (Collegeville, MN: Liturgical Press, 1993).

faith where our spirit awaits our consent to unite with the heart of Christ. It is past words and part of our spiritual capacity. We can do this because of our faith in the Resurrection and our absolute trust in God's love for us. We open our heart and our love connects with Jesus' love for us, and we are drawn to open our heart further. In our faith, we give up our sins and the debris of sin to the One Body of Christ, so when we unite spiritually with the heart of Christ, we unite with love alone—never suffering. It is our suffering that we give up to the Lord in this union of love.

As we open our heart to receive love, we come to believe that we are loved. We find our own desire to love is lit and growing, and we uncover the fears and remorse of sin that have kept our hearts in disguise and not entirely open to receive love. We are led to trust in a depth of God's love and goodness that we never imagined. As we grow in our capacity to receive God's love and the love of others, our heart is set free to love in union with Christ's love. Like each of the missions, the Love-Seeking Mission is one that we grow in until the moment of death. Many people who participate in Transformation of the Heart retreats find a new or renewed experience of knowing Jesus' presence within—and in this love there is great peace and trust to open to the forgiveness work that awaits us.

The Love-Sharing Mission. The Love-Sharing Mission is where we deepen our capacity and strengthen our resolve to love the Lord. This mission includes the meaning and practice of what it is to give our love to Jesus, and how through conversion from sin and in love through Christ, we become adept at love for all neighbors. This mission is central to our capacity to love and receive love and to fulfill our life purpose in Christ. As we engage in this daily prayer practice, we see that in our deepening love for Christ, we are drawn ever closer to the Lord. Jesus shows us the truth of what lies in our way— we are led toward purity of heart. This section is rooted in the Great Commandment: To love the Lord with all of our heart, spirit, and soul. The door to understanding our own needs for recovery from sins (our own and those of others against us) is opened in the union of our love for the Lord and his presence of love and compassion for us. We gain self-compassion and the capacity to forgive others and ourselves. We are called not to subdue our passions to love, but to open to the enormity of Jesus' love and to welcome our heart's increased experiences of peace and justice. Above all, we learn to love our neighbor as ourselves, in Christ's love. As we gain speed in this mission, we also come to know a deeper and more expressive love with those most intimate in our lives, and others more easily receive our love.

Healing begins with the Great Commandment to love the Lord with all of our heart, our spirit, and our mind—and in our contemplation on this commandment alone, much is opened in our heart and the Lord draws us to a deeper desire to love him. The heart is further awakened to Scripture and drawn to the Word of God for wisdom and knowledge of the heart's needs. Love underlies all that happens in this healing prayer, and it is in the heart's return to love—even in the face of adversity, sin, and suffering—where the person is shown the enormity and goodness of the love of God, who desires that all truth be shown to the heart for healing and reconciliation with the Lord.

The Lord leads us to the interior of our heart

St. Benedict teaches us to hear with "the ear of the Heart" when we are in our inner room of prayer. In contemplative practices, oftentimes one is asked to let go of any emotions or thoughts and simply to return to a sacred word that holds meaning. The idea is to empty oneself and to receive God's presence and grace. Many people feel the presence of God's grace in contemplative prayer, and a great deal of healing happens that may or may not be defined in any detail. Even in ten days of contemplative silence, I often knew what needed healing; I could see the knowledge and wisdom about my conversion from sin and harm done to me by others. The Lord has been my teacher in how the heart is transformed, and to see my own disguises of truth, so that I could help others to unwind the truth of their heart. This work has led me to grace in prayer, and to a deeper desire for the Sacraments of Reconciliation and the Eucharist.

With Transformation of the Heart, we are not only seeking grace, we are seeking wisdom—the truth of our heart's healing needs—and that nearly always includes some form of forgiveness that we cannot know without grace. The human heart holds many disguises from sin, and we need Jesus' help to prayerfully pinpoint our own heart's healing needs.

Two hearts are transformed in a Transformation of the Heart healing journey: our own, and the heart of Jesus Christ. Jesus' love is all-inclusive; no one is left out in the cold. As we come near to Jesus' heart, surrendering to our own healing needs, the One Body of Christ is also further united, strengthened, and healed.

The "heart" is at the center of an individual's human life—the center of self—and it holds many meanings in the Old and New Testaments. The Hebrew words for heart, *leb, lebab*, appear about eight hundred times in the Old Testament and are used figuratively to refer to a person's inner life. Numerous examples carry overtones of psychological well-being.[3]

The heart is the center of one's relationship with God. It is the heart that speaks to God (Ps 27:8), trusts in God (Ps 28:7), and receives God's word (Deut 30:14). God knows the secrets of the heart, and can give hearts understanding. Ultimately the renewal of the heart will depend on God's action.

In the New Testament, the Greek word *kardia* is the common translation for leb and lebab and has the same range of meaning as its Hebrew counterparts. Most especially, it represents the inner self (1 Pet 3:4). It is the source of one's deepest motivation and desires (Matt 6:21; Luke 12:34).[4] As the apostle Paul says in Acts 2:37, the heart can be moved to conversion.

The heart is the center of one's relationship with God.

Thus, our heart is the centerpiece of our being and is very much the central point where healing and conversion from sin begin. When we speak of healing and conversion from sin, it is God who is doing the healing, and we are invited to participate. The primary way we participate is to consent to respond to our heart's yearning and longing to love God. As we seek to understand the nature of this longing in ourselves, we are drawn close to the heart of Christ so we can heal. As our love deepens, so does our faith.

---

3 Order of St. Benedict, *The Collegeville Pastoral Dictionary of Biblical Theology* (Collegeville, MN: Liturgical Press, 1996).

4 Ibid.

Sin and the remorse resulting from sin held in our physical bodies cause great ill health to our heart and the rest of our body. As our heart is healed, so are our body, mind, and spirit. We cannot assume perfect health as a result of healing our heart—but we can be certain some healing will occur.

The Resurrection of the Lord is the foundation for this healing paradigm, as it was Jesus' heart of love that was united with the Father's love and given to each of us through the power of the Resurrection. The Holy Spirit is our source of healing—one with the Father and the Son. In the Apostle Paul's prayer in his letter to the Ephesians, he captures the essence of the Triune God and the healing capacity of Christ through our heart:

> *For this reason I bow my knees before the Father,*
> *from whom every family in heaven and on earth takes its name.*
> *I pray that, according to the riches of his glory,*
> *he may grant that you may be strengthened in your inner being*
> *with power through his Spirit, and that Christ may dwell in your*
> *hearts through faith, as you are being rooted and grounded in love.*
> *I pray that you may have the power to comprehend,*
> *with all the Saints, what is the breadth and length and height and*
> *depth, and to know the love of Christ that surpasses knowledge,*
> *so that you may be filled with all the fullness of God.*
> *Now to him who by the power at work within us*
> *is able to accomplish abundantly far more than all we can ask or*
> *imagine, to him be glory in the church and in Christ Jesus to all*
> *generations, forever and ever* (Eph 3:14-21).

As the truth of our heart is shown to us, we come to see the intricacies of two interconnected paths—seeking to grow in our love for Jesus and, at the same time, becoming more aware of Jesus' unconditional love for us. In *The Confessions of St. Augustine*, St. Augustine writes beautifully about how his heart finds God's love.

> *Too late have I loved you, O Beauty so ancient and so new, too late have I loved you! Behold, you were within me, while I was outside: it was there that I sought you, and, a deformed creature, rushed headlong upon these things of beauty which you have made. You were with me, but I was not with you. They kept me far from you, those fair things which, if they were not in you, would not exist at all. You have called to me, and have cried*

out, and have shattered my deafness. You have blazed forth with light, and have shone upon me, and you have put my blindness to flight! You have sent forth fragrance, and I have drawn in my breath, and I pant after you. I have tasted you, and I hunger and thirst after you. You have touched me, and I have burned for your peace.[5]

It is possible to find the depth and beauty of our love for God because the heart of Jesus resides in each one of us; there is a route to the heart of Christ that is uniquely ours. We can seek to understand and to experience this love in our personal prayers and in the Liturgy of the Mass. Worshipping Jesus, praising his name, and offering gratitude for our healing are all ways to enter close to the heart of Christ in prayer.

When we seek to give our love to Jesus, I sense that he returns our love ten-thousand-fold. When we receive this love, we understand that it has a purpose—to heal our heart and soul. As we open our heart to the Lord, we increasingly trust that Jesus' love is for each of us individually, as well as for all others. Many people don't fully take it to heart that Jesus' love is for them, too. Jesus' love is always all-inclusive—there in our joys and in our deepest suffering. Scripture reveals that Jesus never excluded anyone.

> *In the Love-Seeking Mission, we will bump into our own beliefs about our unworthiness to love Jesus.*

> *Everything that the Father gives me will come to me, and anyone who comes to me I will never drive away; for I have come down from heaven, not to do my own will, but the will of him who sent me* (John 6:37-38).

We may need reminders from time to time of Jesus' love for us as we continue on our healing journey. In the Love-Seeking Mission, we will bump into our own beliefs about our unworthiness to love Jesus. When—not if—this happens, we can enter into a loving embrace with Jesus and receive his love. These words often come to my heart in prayer, both for myself and for others: "The Kiss of the Holy Spirit is upon you." Can you look into Jesus' eyes and kiss him on the forehead? If you are tempted to stand back and not give your

---

5 Ibid.

affection, ask Jesus to help you understand what lies in the way. He knows our heart's suffering and heals us one step at a time.

The Lord leads us to trust

Not fully trusting in the Lord's love for us goes hand in hand with the fears that reside in our hearts. Being afraid to love the Lord has its roots in fears of our own offenses against the Lord, or offenses by others against us. Both require forgiveness and love. When you are afraid to love Jesus, ask Jesus to help you examine your conscience. What you find may surprise you. No matter what the offense, you will also be shown the greatest love you have ever known, the greatest compassion you have ever known. Remember, it is Christ who takes action and in grace lifts from you what needs healing. You may well be led back to the circumstances that hurt your heart and led to your own offenses against Jesus. Jesus has compassion, and leads us to self-compassion and understanding of our own weaknesses.

Being afraid to love the Lord has its roots in fears of our own offenses against the Lord, or offenses by others against us.

As we face challenges with forgiveness—forgiving others and forgiving ourselves—we remember the source of love and faith: God.

> *This is the revelation of God's love for us,*
> *that God sent his own Son into the world that we might have life*
> *through him. Love consists in this: it is not we who loved God,*
> *but God loved us and sent his Son to expiate our sins.*
> *My dear friends, if God loved us so much,*
> *we too should love each other* (John 4:9-11).

What we cannot forgive on our own, we cannot love, so we seek God's grace. In God's grace we are healed, one step at a time.

When we seek forgiveness of sins from God, it is our own heart we seek the truth from, and it is the heart of Christ that teaches us the whole truth of our offenses, or perhaps the offenses against us. In either case, it is the heart of Christ that endeavors to enlighten our mind and spirit to reach a state of peace and justice. In my need for forgiveness, I have learned to receive the heart of Christ in interior prayer and to receive blessings of love so that I can be healed. This at times has been made difficult by my own desire for completion, where my sense of justice was premature and more of the story was to unfold through Christ. To fully love our neighbor, we must come to terms with the truth of our own heart and the truth as seen by the heart of Christ within us—and that truth is love itself. The truth about love can be the most painful of all, yet that is where we find peace. It is not love itself that is painful, but the awareness of what has been missed in human relationship.

In the process of learning to forgive, we can get trapped in our inability to trust in God's love. We may recognize that loving and trusting have led to abandonment in the past. If we fear abandonment, it can be hard to trust in the Lord's love—yet if we ask for help from the Lord, it will come in abundance. I believe the fear of abandonment by those we love is our deepest fear and also part of the human condition. We can take our deepest hurts to the Lord. Learning to trust in God's love for us is a critical part of the spiritual journey.

As we learn to love God in fullness, we learn to love ourselves. This is the greatest gain in our healing journey, and it prepares us to share in God's love and to share in the gifts we are able to give others. The simple ways that we care for one another become grace-filled blessings, and we learn to love others through Christ's love for us.

For myself, first and foremost in the Love-Seeking Mission was my gratitude to the Lord for showing me the enormity of his love and his suffering, which led to the healing of my own offenses. My gratitude, love, and faith snowballed at the pace I was being healed.

My sense of remorse unfolded as I sensed that Jesus held and comforted me. This included feelings of suffering that I had held tightly in my heart for decades. Releasing remorse was painful; the armor of the heart's disguise is powerful—but not much of a challenge for God. For many of us, our sins against the Lord include times when we were unable to give or receive love with truth in our heart, and this inability to love with compassion results in sin in our thoughts, words, and deeds.

As I sensed that Jesus took my hand and heart, I knew the words in my heart from the Virgin Mary, "My Son desires to heal your heart," and then I knew Jesus' words in my heart, "I desire to heal all hearts."

I have felt the enormity of Jesus' love and the Blessed Virgin's love for me as I have prayed for the healing of the One Body of Christ. This was not a one-time event, but on numerous occasions I needed to release remorse that constricted my heart. I don't think that I'm unusual in this respect, but that this is the condition of many hearts today—we are unable to give and receive the fullness of love.

Part of understanding and healing the heart's remorse is accepting our responsibility and then releasing our guilt and sorrow about what led to these sins. Jesus wants us to see the entire truth. I believe that the Lord wishes for us to understand how our own faults have caused us to experience a great depth of suffering.

At the same time that we let go of our suffering and remorse, we come to understand self-compassion—perhaps for the first time. The Lord has a way of getting underneath our suffering, lifting it away from us, and showing us our journey to justice. Our surrender makes room for Jesus to give us his gifts of divine mercy, compassion, and love. Human suffering from sin runs deep today in many people, yet I trust Jesus desires to heal all sins.

The greatest act of love is God the Father's sharing of his son with humanity: his passion, death, and resurrection and the sharing of his love in the Eucharist. We can be no closer to God than in his presence in the Eucharist, with our heart open for this communion of love, always remembering our faith. As we notice the reverence in the preparation of the Sacrament, we open our heart to receive the gift of eternal love. Our heart is united in love with the heart of Christ for the fullest communion of love to be made known to us. As we open our heart to Christ, give thanks and express our love to him—our love becomes part of the preparation where the One Body is made whole and poured out to the world.

> *While they were eating, Jesus took a loaf of bread, and after blessing it he broke it, gave it to the disciples, and said, "Take, eat; this is my body." Then he took a cup, and after giving thanks he gave it to them, saying, "Drink from it, all of you; for this is my blood of the covenant, which is poured out for many for the forgiveness of sins. I tell you, I will never again drink of this fruit of the vine until that day when I drink it new with you in my Father's kingdom"* (Matt 26:26-29).

As we receive the Eucharist, we remember Jesus' passion, death, and resurrection—and we hand over our heart to Jesus. As we love Christ, our heart is drawn deeper to the mysteries of his love and we surrender to God's will. As we desire to love and are loved, grace pours out to the world.

As Pope Benedict XVI so beautifully conveys to us:

> God not only offers us his love in the sacraments, in the faith of the Church, but also by placing on our paths people who have been touched by him and who transmit his light. He was the first to live out this love, and he knocks at the door of our hearts in so many ways, seeking to stir up our love in response.[6]

As we experience the Love-Sharing Mission, we share in Jesus' love so that all people may be healed from sin. Thomas Aquinas believed that through desire itself, we could receive the Eucharist, when it was unavailable to us otherwise.

> We can be changed into Christ and become incorporated in him by our desire, even without receiving the Eucharist sacramentally. We receive the Eucharist through desire and are commanded to receive it (John 6:53) *at least through desire.*[7]

The Love-Sharing Mission also includes understanding our own unique gifts of the Holy Spirit, and how we can use them to care for one another as we serve God. We are each called to exercise the fullness of the gifts that we have been given. As we heal, we strengthen our gifts, expand our service, and heal in unity with the Body of Christ. The Apostle Paul calls us to unity through the giving of our gifts:

> But each of us was given grace according to the measure of Christ's gift.The gifts he gave were that some would be apostles, some prophets, some evangelists, some pastors and teachers, to equip the Saints for the work of ministry, for building up the body of Christ (Eph 4:7-11).

---

6 Benedict XVI, *God is Love, Deus Caritas Est.* (San Francisco: Ignatius Press, 2006).

7 Mary Ann Fatula, *Thomas Aquinas: Preacher and Friend* (Collegeville, MN: Liturgical Press, 1993).

It is difficult to engage in this depth of union with God's love or to fully know our gifts, unless our heart and soul are cleansed. Most of us regularly need to approach the Lord for forgiveness. The Lord is always present with divine mercy.

I came to the Lord as a sinner in great need, with a heart harmed by others. I was not and never will be in an "elite" status by any means. Yet Jesus has healed my heart to a great extent, and I have seen the results in my body, mind, and spirit. I have gained psychological and emotional strength, and my immune system has been strong—I rarely have any minor illnesses. I have been cancer-free for 17 years. Although I know this is no guarantee for perfect health in the future, my physical, mental, and spiritual health are greatly improved. I trust that the strength of God's love in healing our heart and soul, has a direct effect on the health and well-being of the physical body—yet this is not "seen" and not easily described; it is healing from the inside out, healing all that is God's will and in God's perfect order. This healing is rooted in our faith and trust in God's love being fully present in all of Creation. As I heal, I have a greater capacity to unite with the heart of Christ in prayer for others, and I experience a greater joy in unconditional love for them. I have learned the meaning of love in friendship, how to love others and how to receive love. I know a greater capacity to love others with tenderness and the joy that is present in this renewed love in myself, and an ever-growing intimacy and tenderness of love in my marriage. I sense a freedom to give and receive love that feels like the presence of eternal love.

St. Therese of Lisieux so eloquently spoke: "How true it is that God alone knows the secrets of our heart!"[8] The Lord indeed sees what we have lost and in God's goodness, love itself fills our heart where harm used to lie; in grace we see our own truth and we are led to deeper truths of the Gospel as it relates to our lifestyle, choices, and life purpose.

Jesus draws us to all truth so that we may have peace and we may more fully love and serve the will of God the Father on earth. This work prepares us well for the Kingdom of Heaven upon our physical death.

---

[8] John Beevers, Translator, *The Autobiography of St. Therese of Lisieux: The Story of a Soul* (New York: Image Books/Doubleday, 2001).

Five: Transformation of the Heart Healing Paradigm

If you love me, you will keep my commandments.
And I will ask the Father, and he will give you another Advocate,
to be with you forever. This is the Spirit of truth,
whom the world cannot receive,
because it neither sees him nor knows him.
You know him, because he abides with you,
and he will be in you. I will not leave you orphaned;
I am coming to you (John 14:15-18).

What lies between your heart and peace with the Lord? What truths have you yet to discover? Perhaps the greatest challenge lies in our accepting of our own truth. We are more accustomed to hiding from truth, especially when it hurts. God helps us to strengthen our trust in his merciful love, so that with the help of the Holy Spirit, we have the courage to acknowledge the truth as we know it and to seek forgiveness and healing of the One Body of Christ. We need not fear the truth, because we trust that the Holy Spirit is present in our heart and much larger than any of our suffering.

Jesus draws our heart to love, to truth, and to remorse—never to despair. If we sense a great deal of shame or despair, we must return immediately to the heart of Christ and the Holy Spirit's intercession in our healing. Jesus will always lift us from our suffering with love, compassion, and understanding of our needs. Our only task in suffering is to let it go at the foot of the Cross, remembering our faith in the Resurrection of the Lord and the institution of the Eucharist. We are healed one small step at a time as we allow ourselves to fall into the arms of the Lord. Jesus never gives us more truth than we can handle. As we pray, we allow our Spirit and our entire being to be risen in Jesus' love.

Jesus draws us to all truth so that we may have peace and we may more fully love and serve the will of God the Father on earth.

For many people, lost love is the circumstance of the heart that is most in need of healing—and bungled relationships are the most difficult truth to face. How do you enter a conversation with Jesus about a loved one who is now missing from your heart? What cause is there to separate oneself from love? Jesus shows us that love is ever present, even when it is covered up by pain and suffering caused by sin. Love is never lost; it is only hidden or disguised. Deceit in one's heart is often from the loss of love—either a loss of love given or received—this can be from childhood or from adulthood.

The courage to seek forgiveness when you feel desolation in your heart is a challenge that can be undertaken. You may experience sadness and sorrow for what is lost, or you may imagine what might have been if truth, rather than fear, had ruled the relationship. Jesus knows the intricacies of the heart and will help you return to your heart's truth many times; the unfolding of truth happens in small steps.

How do you enter a conversation with Jesus about a loved one who is now missing from your heart?

The next chapter includes more information that may help you to integrate the three missions of Transformation of the Heart into your own prayer practice.

Chapter Six

Transformation of the Heart Prayer: How to Begin

The potential for human wholeness—or, in other frames of reference: divine union, liberation, transformation, enlightenment, nirvana— is present in every human person.[1] Father Thomas Keating

"Transformation of the Heart" is expressed in three healing forms: 1) Transformation of the Heart as an individual contemplative practice; 2) healing hands prayer rooted in Transformation of the Heart theology; and 3) a retreat series geared toward healing of the heart during specific liturgical times of the year (such as Advent/Nativity of the Lord or Lent/Easter), where healing of the heart is tied directly to the Gospel. In all three forms, Jesus teaches us to pray as we enter into the silence of intention to love him, and to receive his love for us.

---

1 Thomas Keating, *Contemplative Outreach News: Silence, Solitude, Service* 25, No. 2 (June 2010).

This section explains how to begin a contemplative Transformation of the Heart prayer practice. There are many more intricacies of healing in Jesus' love and prayer that I have written in *The Journey of the Soul: Lessons of God's Healing Love* (a book in progress).

Transformation of the Heart is a contemplative form of prayer. If you are already familiar with that form of prayer—or better yet, have a daily prayer practice—consider adding these elements to your current practice. These steps should also be useful to those who are just beginning a contemplative prayer practice. If you are a beginner, I recommend that you take a workshop in Lectio Divina and centering or contemplative prayer, and that you receive spiritual direction on a regular basis as well. Although Jesus is your primary teacher, there is a lot to be gleaned from your experience spoken and listened to, and the experience and wisdom of others.

The Lord teaches us to pray and leads us in prayer, yet these steps and guidelines may be helpful for getting started. This is how I pray, though each prayer period varies. Prayer is not a rigid event; it is God's way and, as we learn to surrender to the Lord, our prayer practice becomes our own.

This is a contemplative practice that is centered in the gifts of the Holy Spirit that reside in each and every person. The gifts of discernment of Spirit and wisdom and knowledge of God's love are gifts of the Holy Spirit that are within our being and come alive in prayer—unique to each person, as we open our hearts to love the Lord in prayer. For some, the awareness is a simple peace and love—a knowing that God's grace is present. For others, there may be divine revelations about one's growth in faith or need for healing. This awareness often grows with the practice of contemplative prayer, where our heart grows closer to the heart of Christ, and where we become more aware of God's word in us. Spiritual guidance is always useful for anyone who engages in contemplative practice.

Begin your Transformation of the Heart prayer practice by establishing a time and place in your home or church where you have daily access to prayer. You want privacy with no interruptions, and a few sacred items that suggest a holy and reverent atmosphere. Set a prayer time that works for you—I suggest early morning before sunrise and again in mid to late afternoon. The afternoon prayer can be shorter, but it is time for you to be centered in God's love for you, filling you with grace and reminding you to bless all others. For those who pray the Divine Office, you may choose one or two of those prayer periods to enter into silence following the office readings/psalms.

1. Address the Lord directly. Open your heart and offer your love to Jesus. Love the Lord with all of your heart, your mind, your soul—is first and foremost in your prayer. Jesus will draw the sincere heart to the "desire to love." Consent not only to love Jesus, but to allow the Lord to draw your heart to an even deeper desire to love him. Eventually, you will give over your entire heart to the Lord; this is a gift of the Holy Spirit in you. Healing is made manifest when you love Jesus.

2. Do a Lectio reading of a Gospel or another scripture for that day or for the following weekend liturgy. Your heart will awaken to the heart of Christ through the reading of Scripture. *The Word is made manifest in you through love.*

3. Open your heart a step further, and ask the Lord to help you receive his love for you. Embrace the truth of God's love for you and open your heart to receive his love. As you are loved, you will find it safe to trust in your heart's wisdom of truth, shown to you by the Holy Spirit. You will be more aware of God's love for you than your own love for Jesus—because God's love is larger than creation. It takes time to trust in the enormity of this love.

4. In a contemplative silence, allow Jesus to draw you closer to him, noticing that your heart is given away to the Lord, and that you are surrendered to a place of receiving his love for you. In this divine union of love, receive divine wisdom of your own heart's truth. The Lord has not only divine wisdom, but divine intention that is exactly the same for each person. It is my understanding that the Lord's single track of intention is to support your journey toward purity of heart—that is, to remove all deceit in your heart and to fill the places of darkness with love and light. We know when purity of heart is ours, as the Lord will show each heart with perfect clarity where the desire to love Jesus is united perfectly with Jesus' desire to love us. This is a moment of grace, where the Lord raises us to heightened experiences of grace, where we may know the fullest union of God's love—not only for ourselves but also for the sake of the Kingdom.

The heart's journey happens in very small steps, because that is all the human condition can handle and cope with in any single prayer. Disregard your own self-interests and turn to the Lord's intention of purity of heart, and God's will in the moment for you to hear with the "ear of your heart." You may notice emotions, thoughts, images, or even a "knowing" of wisdom of your heart's truth.

5. Mindful hearing, not mindless hearing. Try not to engage in mindless hearing, but in mindful hearing of the Word of God. In loving union with Jesus' love, Jesus indeed has something to say worth paying attention to. If you are not in a prayerful place of divine union of love with Jesus, what you hear may be your own musings, imagination, or even an attempt to get something your way. We are not seeking to have our own way but to hear God's way.

Do not indulge yourself in misery or despair ever, but seek Jesus' assistance if misery strikes. A prayer might be:

"Jesus, please come to my assistance and help me to let this go at the foot of the cross. As I let go of this in your love, please fill my heart and entire being with your love. Leave me only with your love for it is you that I love. I trust in your love for me. Thanks be to God."

As Christians we offer our suffering to Jesus at the foot of the Cross and recognize Jesus' absolute love for us—and in this loving embrace, we praise God's name for his merciful love and the presence of the Holy Spirit in us. We may recognize debris of sin leaving our body as we pray for the healing of the One Body of Christ and give thanks. As Jesus takes the suffering from our heart, and we release whatever emotions lie there, we surrender to Jesus who fills that piece of our heart and our body with his absolute love for us, love that is larger than all of Creation itself. Allow the Holy Spirit to open your heart to one small piece of truth at a time—never unwind a large painful story all at once. The heart holds a lot of debris of sin and harm done to us; the Lord works in small pieces of truth. If you feel you need psychological support as well, seek this kind of professional help. For

Allow the Holy Spirit to open your heart to one small piece of truth at a time—never unwind a large painful story all at once.

many people, the heart's healing is made complete in this prayer form, without need for further psychological therapy. I recommend spiritual direction for all who are on a journey to a closer relationship with the Lord. Hope lies in this healing journey for each person—hope for the miseries of the heart to be healed.

1. Give thanks to God the Father, the Son, and the Holy Spirit. Rest in God's love for you while you say simple prayers, such as: "Glory be to the Father, to the Son, and to the Holy Spirit, One God forever and ever. Thanks be to God. Amen." We always leave prayer knowing God's love for us, and opening our heart to receive his love.

2. After your prayer, you may further witness your healing story. Some people write in a journal, compose poetry, draw, or simply walk in nature. The goal of this after-prayer work is: To clarify your own small piece of truth, to identify forgiveness issues (to forgive yourself or to forgive others), to give praise and gratitude to the Lord, to let go of debris of sin (perhaps recognizing a need for the Sacrament of Reconciliation), and to recognize that both your own love and God's love immerse all of who you are. You will recognize a deeper love for the Lord.

3. Consider your prayer experience and your love for the Lord, *and know that the Lord invites you to a deeper receptivity to his love in the liturgy of the Mass and in the Sacraments.* Give thanks to God for the healing and grace already given in the Sacraments of the Church.

Transformation of the Heart is a contemplative practice, not a single prayer. The more we practice, the more we see ourselves moving forward in our spiritual journey—and most of all, we find ourselves getting closer to the Lord in our faith, and closer to knowing the truth of our life purpose.

Chapter Seven

Two Personal Healing Stories

Grace, mercy, and peace will be with us,
from God the Father and from Jesus Christ, the Son of the Father,
in truth and love (2 John 1:3).

Here are two personal healing stories from retreats at St. Benedict's Monastery in Snowmass, Colorado. Part of the excitement of going to this wonderful place is the combination of season and location—it sits on top of the Rocky Mountains, and both of my visits occurred in the cold of winter. But the biggest draw of Snowmass for me is that it is a community of monks who have made life commitments to God, and I appreciate the deep devotion.

Both of these stories show the three "seeking missions" active in my healing. In the first story, I was called to surrender myself and trust in Jesus' love—it was one of those opportunities to heal where Jesus got my immediate attention. The second is a story of the courage necessary to accept the truth of my heart.

A Healing Story—My Consent to Live and to Love

With a clear jolt, I awoke during the night in my small room at the Monastery, seeing an image in my mind's eye of Christ's death on the cross. The words "Resurrected Spirit" were burning in my heart—I knew God's love was well with me, but I was terrified. I was afraid to look inside of me and see what needed healing; however, I also knew that God was inviting me to consent to the resurrection of my own spirit. I looked around the room and saw my roommate asleep. Somehow it comforted me slightly that I wasn't completely alone. I might have awakened her for company, but as she didn't speak English, I let her sleep. I tried instead to avoid the disturbing image and fall back asleep, but with each effort to slide into unconsciousness I again experienced a jolt of awareness.

After getting only short periods of sleep, I finally got up around 4:30 a.m. No one else in the retreat house was awake. I slipped into long underwear and several layers of clothing and let myself out to walk down the dark icy road lit only by the night stars. All I could hear was the crunch of my boots in the snow.

I looked toward the mountains and impatiently yelled at God, "Okay, I came all this way—what do you want from me?" After this bold, angry demand, I began to cry. With my tears, I surrendered to the presence of God's love and God's desire for my healing. I felt as though I had sunk on my knees into the snow, ice, and earth, though I remained standing. To this day, I recall my boots crunching in the ice.

I truly felt loved and consoled, as God's words burned into my heart: "Do you consent to live? At your birth you were greatly challenged."

I instantly felt the anguish of my soul reaching out to God for love. I cried as I replied, "Yes, I consent to live." I wasn't crying because of the circumstances of my birth, I was crying because of God's goodness and loving presence. I released the anguish to God and felt an incredible consoling love—all of my anxiety and fear dissipated.

During that day, I watched my consent extend as I allowed God to love me, allowed myself to love God, and I opened to God's desire that my heart be transformed.

Later the same day, Father Thomas Keating presented the four consents via videotape: the consent to live, the consent to a spiritual journey, the consent to know that life is basically good, and the consent to death (literal death as well as death of the false or unhealthy self). I was struck by the synchronicity between my nighttime experience and the retreat presentation. A piece of truth was emerging: this is an example of the Lord leading me in the truth-seeking mission. I began to understand that an element had been lacking; that in some way, I had not at birth given my consent to live. That consent, however, was necessary for my overall healing.

During this healing, I did not know or remember any specifics of my birth. I did, however, experience fear, which was very real. This fear was released as I consented; and in my consent, I received the love of the Lord and breath by the Holy Spirit. I knew something very challenging had been lifted from me in grace.

For me, this healing was not only about the consent to live, but my willingness to trust in love as well. The anguish and jitters in my heart were gone. Each night thereafter, I slept in God's peace, aware of God's divine mercy and real presence in me. This was a watershed healing.

A Healing Story—"She said . . ."

For a 50th birthday present to myself, I signed up for a ten-day silent contemplative retreat at St. Benedict's. Having been on a spiritual journey for several years, I was seeking a deeper adventure into my own soul. So I flew to Denver and then drove two hours across a beautiful mountain pass to Old Snowmass.

On the first full day, following Mass, a teacher surfaced. Father Theophane Boyd (who passed away in 2003) stood in the vestibule in his long robes, hunched over farther than what appeared normal. I thought he must be old. Later I learned he had a severe form of arthritis and wasn't nearly as old as he appeared.

I asked him if he had any advice for me. He generously welcomed me to sit down in a small chair, next to his desk, which was piled up many times over with books. He searched for a Buddhist book that included the story of the "Absolute Mountain." Not finding the book, he proceeded to tell me the story. It goes, as I recall, something like this:

> *The absolute mountain contains all of the grandeur of God's strength and holiness. It withstands all weather, all people, and, most of all, all of God's animals' droppings. Nothing can threaten it, so it has no fear, only strength. Visualize the mountain's glory in your mind. Now hold onto that vision of strength and pray.*

He began to quiz me a bit. I felt as if he wasn't really listening to me as much as he was trying to figure out what to say next. As I began speaking, he said, "Stop talking. Begin your sentences with 'She said' . . ."

I didn't like the idea of speaking in the third person, but I felt commanded to try it, so I did. Almost immediately as I spoke "She said . . ." I began crying.

He muttered, "Just like a woman."

We both laughed, and our visit soon ended. I went outside, grabbed my pen, and stood before the snow-covered mountain. These words flowed through me in God's grace. Even the shape of "the Word" looks like a mountain.

She said . . .

She wonders why her?
So hurt?
So loved?
So many graces?
So arrogant in others' eyes?
So sorrowful?
So open to God's love?
So open to His will?
How can she love God so tenderly?
How can she be in His presence without fainting from His love?
How can it be His joy for her life?
How can she not be one with Christ in every breath?
How can she not offer others what they need?
How can she not see her body as whole?
How can she not see her beauty as whole?
How can she not dance more with life?
How can she not love that arm, and breast that is missing?
How can she not know how beheld she is?
How is she to love God now that He has given her so much?
How does she speak of His love so tender of her?
Does she not know to let be the definition of love and to just receive

with all her might?
Does she not know the absolute mountain holds gems and treasures of
His love for her?
Does she not allow the golden sky to reverberate His love upon her?
Does she not see the glimmering mountain edge invite
her love to be revealed?
Does she now see the grandeur of His beauty and love?

Father Theophane's lesson set the stage for an amazing ten days with the Lord. I have given the image of the Absolute Mountain to many.

My heart's journey has been a daily practice of healing, as in these stories. Most days it comes in small steps, but always it is filled with the love and guidance of the Holy Spirit, both for my study and for my work. Living with the fullness of love is the topic of the next section.

Chapter Eight

Healing Hands Prayer

*I made your name known to them,
and I will make it known,
so that the love with which you have loved me
may be in them,
and I in them* (John 17:26).

Each of us has a calling that was given to us at our conception. We have a purpose that includes one or more gifts of the Holy Spirit—and the gifts and lives of each one of us are for the wholeness and wellness of the world. As far as I understand it, the spiritual gifts I have been given include love, wisdom, and knowledge. The Lord has equipped me with these gifts so that I can lay hands on others for healing and help others open their heart to God's love, truth, and need for forgiveness—applying what I have gleaned in the Transformation of the Heart healing paradigm, rooted in God's love and Scripture.

Laying on of hands prayer ministry is as old as the Gospel where Jesus taught the world that he was the divine healer, as he laid hands on and miraculously healed many by their faith. In our faith, and through our prayer, we are called not to perform miracles of healing, but to seek Jesus' intercession and healing for those for whom we pray. Our primary call in these prayers is to love the Lord and to extend our love to the person receiving the prayer—and to seek God's loving grace to heal the person. The purpose of each healing hands prayer is to pray for the person's soul, for their heart to receive God's love, and for whatever they request—for God's will to be served, for the sake of the Kingdom of Heaven.

This chapter includes two segments: 1) a story of my wake-up call by the Lord entitled: The Table is Set, where I was called to provide healing prayers; and 2) the healing prayers inspired by the Holy Spirit.

Wake-up Call: "The Table is Set"

I was seeking God's love during the 2002 contemplative prayer retreat with Father Thomas Keating at Old Snowmass. During an afternoon gathering at the retreat, Father Thomas told the story of Brother Bernie, a long-time resident monk at Old Snowmass who had passed away several years before. I felt drawn to Bernie's story; all of who he was intrigued me. I could see "Bernie's Rock" out the window as Father Thomas spoke.

Bernie was from Massachusetts and joined the Trappist Monk cloister when he was 17. The old culture of the Trappist Monks was quite strict; it has lightened up very little over the years. When Bernie began his Trappist vocation, the culture was one of silence, prayer in chapels, work, and little-to-no opportunity for friendship or service to one another. Bernie's natural instinct was to communicate often with people to see how he could serve them. This was a challenge in the Trappist community, but Bernie found his ways. Over time, he developed and used hundreds of sign language cues. With flamboyant gestures, sometimes using his whole body, he would sign or gesture to communicate when everyone else was silent and avoiding eye contact.

One activity he cashed in on was the opening of doors. He would swing the door wide, bow to the person coming through, and kiss their hand. He learned to cook so he could please people with food, and he instigated ice cream celebrations when few celebrations were allowed. His gift of exuberant hospitality found many ways to show itself. While Father Thomas was talking about Bernie, I recognized my own inclination to provide hospitality and welcoming, and I wished I had known him.

I also loved the "rebel" side of Bernie, who worshipped God with devotion yet never gave up who he was. Father Thomas was often on the receiving end of Bernie's hospitality, with slight irritation at times because Bernie pushed the edges of all of the rules. Bernie also had the gift of knowing the goodness of life. He recognized beauty and wanted to share small things of beauty with others. Bernie is known for one of his beliefs: "Always love what God gives you in the world passionately, and be willing to let it go at a moment's notice." I have returned to the beauty and truth of these words on many occasions.

Bernie loved to pray in nature. He often returned to the same rock to pray, which became known as "Bernie's Rock." As Father Thomas said "Bernie's Rock," I felt my heart jump; this was the Holy Spirit nudging me. Knowing the hike would be a challenge, I asked Brother Chuck to show me the way. Rather than offering to take me, he pointed out the window toward the highest peak, saying there was a rough path part of the way up that was a bit icy, but I could make it if I took my time and wasn't afraid of heights. I was. I looked around and saw one woman left in our gathering room. She was happy to join me in the climb.

Barbara had more hiking experience than I, and she took the lead in bushwhacking our way up to the rock. From the first step, this adventure was a prayer. It was to be a day of silence, so we began that way. The sun was brilliant against the snow. The temperature was in the low 20s, but we warmed up quickly. I noticed traces of bear and saw a few rabbits. About halfway up, we noticed that the trail had all but disappeared. Barbara kept dancing swiftly up the hillside, and I found myself right behind her with little fear of the steep climb. We were both amazed with the ease and pace at which we were "ascending" Bernie's Rock.

As we neared the summit, I broke the silence. "The table is set," I said.

"Huh?" responded Barbara.

I told her God was speaking to my heart. The words were as clear as day to me. We both broke out laughing with awe and joy as we turned and looked at the incredible view, well aware we were standing in God's grace.

At the top, I knew the "banquet of God's love" was before us. We were at God's table of forgiveness. The beauty of creation was before us. It was breathtaking.

There, at the top of the mountain, God welcomed me home to sit at the table of forgiveness, to eat and drink of Jesus' body and blood, and to bring others to his table. The table had been set with all the welcoming detail a table can hold. I became aware of my need to forgive others and to forgive myself. More importantly, I knew "the table of forgiveness" was the work that I was called to do. Fears that lay dormant inside me were released. This time I experienced no suffering, only the warmth of God's love transforming my heart and calling my love to be in union with his for service to others. God's goodness and my trust in God were infinite.

I said a silent prayer in memory of Bernie. I noticed a cross drawn in the fresh snow at the rock's edge, with no footprints leading to it. I stood in awe of the moment, marveling at the depths of God's holy love.

Barbara didn't stop and was busy figuring out an easier way back. Her route included crossing a steep, slippery rock. Barbara ran sure-footedly across the snow-covered rock. In a hurry to catch up, I got down on my butt and tried to slide across it. Slipping a bit, I imagined myself in the center of a landslide. Barbara held out her hand. I grabbed it and walked safely across. As we made our way down, we broke our silence and began swapping stories of our spiritual paths. The synchronicity in our lives was amazing. We knew God's grace had brought us together to witness each other's journey. As we returned to the monastery, our hearts filled with beauty and excitement, it was time for my personal consultation with Father Thomas.

My goal was to tell him of my experiences of sharing love with God, and to ask for any wisdom he wanted to offer. He listened for a while, smiled, and quietly said:

"If you are asking me why you experience so much of God's love, I think you experience it in this fashion because . . . you must need it." There was a long pause. Honestly, I guess I was hoping he would tell me that I was special somehow. Finally, he continued. "Oneness with God in prayer is 'no-thing,' or 'is-ness'—it is a deep surrender to God's love and will; just let it be and remember to pray each morning, and I think in the late afternoon is also of great help. It is God who does all of the work." He asked me many questions about my prayer practice, and appeared well satisfied that God was managing my spiritual growth.

When I returned home, I decided that I wanted spiritual direction from a Roman Catholic priest, and I felt called to study the ancient roots of Catholicism that I was sensing in my soul. I made a blind call to a Benedictine Monastery, having no idea how I would be received. I asked to speak with the one monk whose name I knew, an iconographer. When he answered his phone, I introduced myself and told him I was seeking spiritual direction because I loved God, and I was seeking to find out why I was called so deeply to the Lord's love. I mentioned my educational credentials and 20-year work experience so he wouldn't think I was nuts. He suggested I call a particular "elder" priest who gave spiritual direction. I did, and he invited me to visit.

When we met, I was initially disappointed that he wasn't old. I was seeking safety in any way I could find it, and a very nice old monk sounded good to me. This man was younger than I was, but I decided to stay and talk with him.

He offered to hear my confession, which he introduced by telling me that he was a great sinner. If this was supposed to make me feel better, it did. I told him the story of my entire life—my family history before birth and highlighting times of significance. I had written out a timeline with specific ages where significant events happened. I didn't cry, but when I left, I felt very vulnerable. I had told him EVERYTHING, and I remember thinking: "No worry, I won't ever see him again."

He continued to direct me for ten more years! When I asked him what he thought about the way God was working in me, he said: "This is God's divine mercy." His words were not a complete surprise to me, but God's goodness and mercy were not part of my daily vocabulary, as they are today. He was not judgmental; he showed concern and kindness and gave me a list of books on prayer and many of the early Saints in the mystical prayer tradition, which I enjoyed immensely. After I read everything he gave me, I scheduled more time. I haven't stopped asking him questions yet, and I've read more books. Over the years he has witnessed the gifts of the Holy Spirit in me, and provided much counsel and numerous library books. Spiritual direction for me is like food—I need the nourishment and guidance so that I stay on the right track with God. Laying hands on and praying is one of the ways the Lord has called me, and I continue this practice.

Here is the prayer the Lord gave me for "laying on of hands" of others.

The Baptismal Font of Love

> We open our hearts to your love, dear Lord,
> and offer to you all of our love as we pray for this person's complete healing. We pray first for her/his soul, for forgiveness needs including the debris of sin and harm done by others that underlie bodily healing needs. We acknowledge one Baptism for the forgiveness of sins. We humbly ask you, God the Father, only for what is your will in this prayer. As we seek the abundance of your love, we remember that your desire to love each of us is far greater than what we know in human desire. We give you thanks for your infinite love and wisdom, and for all the healing grace you have shown to us.
> Lord Jesus, please unite our love with yours so that our prayers and faith may be pleasing to you. In following the Greatest Commandment, we offer to you, Lord Jesus, to love you with all of our heart, our spirit, our soul, and with all of our strength.
>
> In remembrance of your suffering, death, and resurrection, we deeply surrender and open our hearts to receive your love with the divinity of your hands over our human hands.
> May your gentleness of touch unite with our desire to love you. Please answer our longing to be near you by drawing our hearts to you, as you show us what is needed in the healing of our own forgiveness needs—including the debris of sin from harm by those who have sinned against us. We surrender to the depth of your love that you call us to, and open our hearts to receive the fullness of this love and your consoling touch.
>
> In the deepest mysteries of your love, we pray for the healing of the Earth as one with your love. In your goodness, we seek the raising of the chalice, the body and blood of our Lord Jesus Christ.

> *In this spiritual receipt of the Eucharist, we pray for the healing of the One Body of Christ. We wish to renew our covenant of love with you for all time. May the kiss of the Holy Spirit be upon us. Blessed be God forever. In the name of the Father, the Son, and the Holy Spirit. Amen.*

I prepare the person receiving the prayer, and others who may be in the room, by introducing these ideas and giving them a copy of the prayer. Often, I will pray most of the prayer in silence. I lead those present in a Scripture reading. The following prayer is spoken directly to the person on whom we will lay hands.

> *Open your heart—to God first loving you,*
> *before the conception of your birth and through all time.*
> *Recognize your heart's longing to love God,*
> *and open to the fullness of this knowing.*
> *In bodily healings, the heart is first touched by God's love*
> *in response to our own longing,*
> *and all healing is of God's will.*
> *Know that you are in God's hands.*
>
> *You must love the Lord your God with all your heart, with all your soul, with all your mind, and with all your strength. The second is this: You must love your neighbor as yourself. There is no greater commandment than these.* (Mark 12:30-31).

Finally, I address words such as these to others present regarding our intentions about the work we are doing together in the name of and through the power of God.

> *We open our hearts to receive God's love,*
> *to recognize our longing to love God,*
> *and to gaze onto the person who is receiving the prayer with love in our hearts.*
> *As we pray, we acknowledge God's infinite mercy*
> *and love for each of us in our healing needs.*
> *As we love God prayerfully, we ask for Jesus' healing touch to be present through our hands, only as is God's will for the healing of the other. We are not "healers"—we are people who pray.*
> *It is our faith and our love for God and for one another that make up this prayer. As we are asked to love God in the Greatest Commandment, we are also healed as is God's will in our "heart,*

soul, mind, and strength." In God's presence, we give thanks in silence.
We all receive blessings in this prayer together.

I invite the person receiving the prayer to sit or lie down in a comfortable position, and to quietly reflect on his or her faith, opening their heart to receive Jesus' love. Often I pray with two or three other people, and we will each lay hands on the person and pray. The prayer is in Jesus' hands. At some point during the prayer, I simply sit down, knowing Jesus' hands are still on the person, and I remain silent in surrender to God's will.

In these prayers, people often ask for physical healing. Because Jesus is a holistic healer, I pray not only for physical healing, but also for healing of the person's soul and for sins to be made known in their heart, for their desire to love Jesus to be made known at deeper levels in their heart, and for healing of the body, mind, and spirit at the will of God the Father. Most people experience a profound sense of grace during the prayer, as they open to God's love and receive the healing touch of Jesus.

I sense a spiritual receipt of the Body of Christ in these prayers. I believe the Eucharist received in the Mass is the most powerful form of God's love and healing to be received. The Lord reminded me of this truth with the inspired words below drawing my heart to the Liturgy of the Mass.

The Eucharist

The Eucharist
The Word
United with my heart
Unfolding all desire
All love
I crumble to the ground
Face down in surrender
Outstretched before the Cross
Jesus responds
With His desire to love me

My Beloved lifts me up
Still lying, in suspension
Absolutely immersed
Above and below
I open my heart once more
With the ends of our fingertips
We touch
Knowing vibrations of love are
The One Body, the One Blood of Christ
Nourishment everlasting. Amen.

Section Three

The Fulfillment of Desire: Oneness with God

Overview

*We love because he first loved us.
In this love, not that we loved God but that he loved us and sent
his son to be the atoning sacrifice for our sins.
There is no fear in love, but perfect love casts out fear;
for fear has to do with punishment
and whoever fears has not reached perfection in love*
(1 John 4:19, 10, 18).

First, he loved us . . . before we were born. This is the beginning of our journey to fulfillment of love. It begins with God who gives us life in the womb, who gives us breath and the longing to love—by the power of the Holy Spirit.

The fulfillment of God's love is the love that is gained eternally, as love that has been lost through sin and injustice against us is healed. In the fulfillment of love, we recognize love and peace as our heart's response to life and to circumstances during our day. Eternal love is with us at our beginning. In this sense, life and death are one. I feel that the difference between eternal love during our life, and eternal love at our death is one thing—it is sin and the disturbance that our heart knows from sin. Sin disturbs the knowing of great peace that is known at death.

In this section, we look at what is given up as we participate in our own healing through the Transformation of the Heart healing journey—what is gained and what is lost? What is the nature of love that is gained? What is the nature of peace that is gained? What is the nature of forgiveness and justice accomplished that is gained? What is the nature of eternal light and infinite love that is gained? What is lost—what is the nature of sin, sorrow, remorse, and debris of sin that is held in the physical body—an underlying cause of many illnesses of the body, mind, and spirit? What does it take to move through layers of deceit of the heart that contains the debris of much sin of our own and of others against us? There is more mystery than not in all of these questions, yet this section explores the tender territory of healing the heart with Jesus Christ, who desires to show his love to each person and who desires to receive love from each person.

The next two chapters explore the nature of eternal life and love, as captured by saints and Scripture—and my own prayerful experiences with the Lord. The last chapter includes a Beatific Vision that God gave to me as a gift during a difficult time of healing for myself. Words cannot express such events, but words do convey some of the beauty and truth of the Eternal Word in the Kingdom.

This section includes three chapters:

Chapter Nine: What is Gained and What is Lost

Chapter Ten: The Eternal Nature of God's Love

Chapter Eleven: A Glimpse of the Kingdom of Heaven

God draws our heart to him in many ways; the most potent force of Jesus' love is in the Eucharist instituted at the Last Supper. Through the Eucharist, Jesus draws us to oneness with himself. Grace opens our heart to our own truth and to understanding truth in the Word. What lies in our heart that blocks the fulfillment of love through the Eucharist? What do we leave behind as we enter into our heart's capacity to love in fullness?

We remember that God the Father first loved us, and we respond by loving Jesus with all of our heart, mind, spirit, and strength—for love's sake and for the sake of our own healing. His merciful love leads us to fully embrace his love, and through our love for Christ, we can fully love others, and we are led by the Lord to eternal life and love.

To come to the fullness of love, we must first examine what lies in our heart that keeps us away. This is the work of Transformation of the Heart.

*Keep your heart with all vigilance,
for from it flow the springs of life* (Prov 4:23).

Chapter Nine

What is to be Gained and What is Lost?

Deep love demands deep conversion.[1]
Thomas Dubay

Harm done to the body, mind, spirit, and soul—whether that harm is done to us or by us—has its roots in the heart. The heart is the center-force of human life. What meaning does any activity have without the heart's participation? The heart's source of energy is the center-force of one's Spirit, the transcendent qualities in each person. This center-force begins at conception and is the Holy Spirit, or the heart of Christ, united with the human heart. When our heart is damaged, our closeness with Spirit suffers.

The heart is the center-force of human life.

What hurts the heart hurts the soul. The soul drives the heart and is united with the heart; each is dependent on the other as long as the body is alive. Upon death, the soul moves on, always attached to the Spirit, the center-force of the heart.

---

1 Thomas Dubay, S.M., *Deep Conversion, Deep Prayer* (San Francisco: Ignatius Press, 2006).

We are whole in the sense that body, mind, spirit, and soul are interconnected, with our heart being the center-force. Wellness is not only about healing the body, mind, and spirit—but is also, and more precisely, about the soul's recovery. So what does our soul need to recover from?

All damage to the heart is held in the soul and in the body. We seek forgiveness from sin—sins done against us, and our own sins. As we give up holding on to the injuries done to our heart, our healing will always include forgiveness on some level. We seek to empty ourselves of sin in God's grace, and we pray for the healing of the other. We might inadvertently hold the burden of the others' sins against us. If we do, that is damaging to our own heart as well. The Lord's response to our prayer is always to lighten our soul. And because the soul governs all else, this lightening affects our body, mind, and spirit, too.

> *All damage to the heart is held in the soul and in the body.*

The psychology of the soul refers to the conscience of the soul. Sin resides where light in the soul is missing. Our soul knows what work is left for us to do while we are alive. We each desire to complete our life's work with the Lord before our death.

In the practice of psychology today, many try to separate the workings of the whole person from the person's spirit, as if the mind operated in a vacuum. You can set all the lifestyle goals and try all the cognitive-behavioral change you like, but unless you include the heart and Spirit, healing and related change will not be complete. It is similar in western medicine—treating only the mind's or body's symptoms of ill health is not likely to succeed completely without the work of the heart, spirit, and soul. Medicine treats from the outside inward, and faith heals from the inside out. I have come to believe faith is the more complete of the two and I rely on each one.

> *I have come as light into the world,*
> *so that everyone who believes in me*
> *should not remain in darkness.*
> *And I, when I am lifted up from the earth,*
> *will draw all people to myself*
> (John 12:46, 32).

In our spiritual healing journey, we are reaching for increased light in our soul. How is it that the glimmer of light in our soul becomes illuminated and rich with the properties of love? Jesus draws us in many ways to our own longing or desire to love him. Our need to see the truth of sin and our need to seek and grant forgiveness are the same as our need to love. Truth and love work hand in hand. The heart and mind must cooperate with each other. God's truth can only be witnessed through divine love, and this love can only be witnessed as we acknowledge the truth about sin in our lives. As we encounter God's love, our heart is nourished with the capacity to love, to trust, and to see the truth—to hold to our faith in the Resurrection of Christ. All are found simultaneously as the glimmer of light is illuminated in our soul.

At times the soul is weighted with sin and knows torments and great misery—I call this the presence of "thunderclouds" where fear is present. While this condition can be explained in many ways, I believe that in the creation of human beings, the soul does have a limit in its creation that perhaps allows for fear—not with the intention of destroying the human body, but to awaken the human body to God's infinite and tender love. When fear is experienced, I believe it is a call to open to God's love and God's healing through truth in the heart. Something lies there—whether it is harm done to a person by another, or another person's remorse or regrets that need healing. Some may experience this knowing of fear to mean that God is angry. I don't think so.

God can only see so much misery in a soul before he brings thunderclouds across it with a different kind of light, a light that strikes the soul with fear. When this happens, it may be to teach the soul to surrender to God's infinite and tender love. Many people have seen the thunder and lightning and wondered what God was so angry about. This is a question for each and every soul to discover. Is God angry, or is it that God desires you to come closer? Do you believe—as your faith tells you—that God's love is all-powerful, powerful enough to heal all anger, all sorrow, all anguish, and all sin?

I have seen the thunderclouds come over my heart and it was not a subtle call. I experienced a great deal of unexplained fear; I immediately asked a friend to pray with me. Following our prayer, she told me that she felt God wanted me to return to the Catholic

Church. She was Buddhist and not accustomed to referring people to the Catholic Church, but told me she felt sure that my experience of the thunderclouds was a call to return. We prayed together in the moment, and my fears were reduced significantly. I returned to the Catholic Church the next day and received the sacraments of Reconciliation and the Eucharist. My recovery in some ways was immediate, yet this ordeal took days to unfold. What I know today is that my heart was in disguise on many levels and the Lord was asking for my attention to unwind the truth and to surrender in my faith—not only to return to the Church, but for eternal life in Christ to be fulfilled in my soul. I was not only being called to forgiveness of sins, I was being called into God's purpose in me—to pray for others—that lay deep in my faith. I was unaware of my needs to forgive others and myself, and to be forgiven by Christ. In my Transformation of the Heart healing journey, Jesus showed me truth and his love. Today, my heart knows love replacing the places of darkness, pain, and fear in my soul.

The root of my distress included the harm that had been done to me by others as well as my own need to forgive. With the blinders raised from my eyes, I have not since doubted my daily prayer journey with Jesus. My gratitude for his merciful love given out to us on the cross is beyond words.

The closer we get to Jesus, the more aware we become that we have very little authority or power on our own. Yet as we unite our love with Jesus' heart, we gain true authority through his truth and love, and we gain strength and power to serve, at his will.

The journey of the heart leads us to an intimacy of love with the Lord, and to an intimacy of love with others. It is God's will for us to trust in the loving intentions of others. If we keep our heart open to love, when a person treats us badly, we are more likely to try to work out the conflict. Avoiding the work of conflict resolution opens the door to broken relationships and to more sin. When we turn away from love, we sin. We may well doubt the love in the heart of the person who harmed us. If someone harms me, how can I trust in their love for me? The answer lies in our faith: underneath all brokenness lies love. When I open to God's love in prayer, I see my love for the person and the person's love for me, and I ask God to lift the sin in

Underneath all brokenness lies love.

myself and I pray for God's truth and reconciliation to be present for both of us.

Transformation of the Heart prayer reminds us to open our heart to receive love. This has not been simple for me. In my healing journey, I have needed to learn how to trust in the love of others and to open my heart to that love. As a result of my healing journey so far, I know an ever-growing tenderness and intimacy in my capacity to love. In my marriage, my husband calls this a "mutuality in marriage" that is a unity and oneness in our love, where we know each other as whole people. We know each other's life stories—healing has happened, and we each are on a spiritual journey in God's love. We love and accept all that is of the other. Our hearts open to each other's love, and we are able to share a deep love that is God's will in the intimacy of our marriage. I know greater tenderness, joy, and peace in loving relationships with close friends as well. I have lost my edge of criticism of others. There is a great deal to be gained in our capacity to give and receive love in the Transformation of the Heart journey, and probably a great deal to be lost (that is just as important). What is lost is also God's will—as what is lost is what permits us to sin against others, sometimes without even being aware of it.

Returning to the heart of Christ, and to my own heart, with many fears and needs for forgiveness released, I have been more able to love Jesus with all of my heart, spirit, soul, and strength. This was not a one-time prayer and release; I pray daily for divine mercy for myself and for the world, and I continue to experience truth and love—which are one and the same for me today. I do not fear truth any more than a person would fear love. None of us complete our healing until the moment of our death, and in the meantime, it is Jesus' transforming action in us that we come to trust.

One of my greatest fears was that my love would be rejected by God and by others. This fear has dissipated, giving me freedom to love Jesus fully and to love others freely. For the first time in my life, I know the true meaning of joy in my heart, and specifically the joy and peace of the fullness of love. I allow love without fear of rejection, and I love others knowing my heart is filled with joy and peace. God has given me a new heart of love, replacing much of my stony heart. When I make mistakes today, I return to the commandment to love Jesus fully. I am often drawn to my love for the other, even if the other person is behaving badly toward me. When I am challenged to see Christ's reflection in a person, I return to prayer and find something in my own conscience that is blocking my sight of the Lord.

I have not only gained love and peace in my heart, I have lost (to one degree or another) many unhealthy behavior patterns. Knowing God's merciful love for all, I have much less temptation to judge others. It is easier for me to love others who are different than I am; I desire to love others and to help in simple ways. I rarely feel angry. I sleep very well, and I experience no anxieties. It no longer frightens me to be with those who are dying; I feel called to the sacred moments of eternal love and life. Naturally, I do have *some* fear of death, but I have a much stronger belief in God's eternal love and life given at our death. No behavioral therapy meant to overcome some of my personal tendencies or habits would have been successful without Jesus' love guiding my spiritual growth. The joy of gaining peace and love is not to be underestimated—it is how the Lord wishes us to live and to love one another.

When there is great darkness in a soul—as is the case for some today—a person may be left wondering where God has gone. People tell me that God is not here, at least not for them. Yet inside each person is a glimmer of light—in some, a distant coal that is barely visible, in others a bright lamppost surrounded by loving elders. God is there the same for each. The call may be subtle or crystal-clear. Longing to more fully understand your life purpose and to give yourself to it is a simple but key example of God's call for you to open your heart to his love. He will show you the truth of your life purpose and heal your heart so you can get on with it. God's love is ever present in the lighting of a soul. God calls your name today and invites you to truth, to love, and to wisdom.

What is gained is love without measure—eternal life and blessings of love on earth—you desire to love all, to bless all, and there is peace in your heart where you know the presence of Christ is with you. You have the freedom to bless others well. My desire and resolve to love God is stronger than ever before, and this is a gift from God, a gift that is for each of us. We can choose to receive God's love, love others, and bless others with each and every breath.

Chapter Ten

The Eternal Nature of God's Love

> When they had finished breakfast, Jesus said to Simon Peter, "Simon son of John, do you love me more than these?"
> He said to him, "Yes, Lord; you know that I love you."
> Jesus said to him, "Feed my lambs."
> A second time he said to him, "Simon son of John, do you love me?"
> He said to him, "Yes, Lord; you know that I love you."
> Jesus said to him, "Tend my sheep."
> He said to him the third time, "Simon son of John, do you love me?"
> Peter felt hurt because he said to him the third time,
> "Do you love me?"
> And he said to him,
> "Lord, you know everything; you know that I love you."
> Jesus said to him, "Feed my sheep" (John 21:15-17).

This appearance of the Lord on the shore of Tiberias was the third witness by the apostles of the Lord's resurrection and, I believe, is instructive of how Peter was to "feed the sheep"—that is, to fully love God. He was asked three times if he loved the Lord; perhaps this question was instructive for not only how to preserve the law but how to ensure forgiveness and eternal life.

No one arrives as an enlightened soul at the feet of the Lord until death. The purpose of our spiritual journey and of our life is, however, as St. John of the Cross stated: There are two goals to life: 1) by grace we offer to God a pure heart (through charity); and 2) we experience divine presence and glory of God in Heaven (possible on Earth).[1]

We learn to do both of these as we deepen our love for God. We become aware of the everlasting nature of God's love, as shown to us in Scripture through the Resurrection and Ascension. Jesus lived, died, rose, and ascended for a purpose—to save each one of us from our sins and to bring us to his eternal love and life. The joy of the Risen Lord is our participation in divine love while on earth, and the fulfillment of love in eternal life. All love we receive is eternal and is healing.

So what is the eternal nature of this love? We look to Scripture, to the saints and mystics for stories passed down about the nature of this love; nonetheless, it is only upon our death that we will know the fulfillment of God's love. We are, however, getting glimpses of eternal love and wisdom through the hearts of mystics, and through the words spoken so beautifully in scripture. The purpose of this chapter is to illustrate what I interpret as the eternal nature of love itself, through others' writings and through my Transformation of the Heart journey with the Lord. Scriptures tell us that "purity of heart" is important to the Lord Jesus Christ, and this purity of heart is directly related to eternal life.

Blessed are the pure in heart; for they will see God (Matt 5:8).

The Lord's gift in the Transformation of the Heart healing paradigm is a framework for healing what lies between sin, the heart of the Trinity (the Father, the Son, and the Holy Spirit), and eternal life. It is our work to complete, as we walk in the footsteps of the Lord and desire to heal our heart. John Cassian, a 4th century monk, reminds us that "purity of heart is a gift, not an achievement.

---

1 Kieran Kavanaugh, O.D.D., and Otilio Rodriguez, O.C.D., Translators, *The Collected Works of St. John of the Cross* (Washington, D.C.: ICS Publications, Institute of Carmelite Studies, 1991).

Still, you must try."[2] Further, he writes that we are helpless without God's grace, yet the soul must participate with Christ. You must exercise your moral judgment, yet you are helpless without Christ. This is the work of Transformation of the Heart: to be a full participant in the truth of your heart and your behavior—past, present, and future—and only through grace will you achieve purity of heart. John Cassian's Conferences are filled with wisdom intended for monks, related to this objective—purity of heart—necessary for sanctification.[3]

> *Therefore, we must follow completely anything that can bring us to this objective, to this purity of heart, and anything which pulls us away from it must be avoided as being dangerous and damaging. After all, it is for the sake of this that we undertake all that we do and all that we endure. . . . With this as our continuous aim, all our acts and thoughts are fully turned toward its achievement, and if it were not ever firmly before our eyes all our efforts would be empty, hesitant, futile, and wasted, and all the thoughts within us would be varied and at loggerheads with one another.*

Healing the heart of one person at a time is also how the earth heals—each sin forgiven is healing to the One Body of Christ, and to Creation itself.

Perhaps the strongest spiritual language used to convey fulfillment of the heart's love is that of a spiritual "marriage" with the Lord, as written by many mystics including St. John of the Cross. Scripture teaches us this love is eternal. The "bride" and "bridegroom" language describes both hearts being freely given to one another, without the weight of sin. We come to a full knowing of delight in the Lord's receipt of our love, as well as a realization of Jesus' love. This intimacy of love with the Lord is what I mean by the beauty of the fulfillment of love—it is the experience whereby God's special self-communication is more alive and intense, and our response to this love is even more intensely alive than human love. St. John of the Cross refers to these moments symbolically as "living flames, delightful wounds, splendors from the lamps of fire, and awakenings

---

[2] Colm Luibheid, Translation and Preface, *John Cassian Conferences* (New York: Paulist Press, 1985).

[3] Ibid.

of the Beloved."[4] I particularly like the phrase "awakenings of the Beloved," as true love is never demanded, but awakened. We have the will in us to actively participate in this love, or not.

These moments are not permanent while we are on earth, but are a glimpse of eternal life. We know only a little about the mysteries of God's love, and wait for death for the eternal mysteries to be made known to us in fullness.

In our desire to love the Lord, we are drawn to a resolve to love Jesus above all other earthly things. Our process for healing requires an intimate relationship with Jesus. As I offer my love to Jesus, my heart is united with the heart of Christ, and I am shown certain truths, certain words that awaken my spirit to a deeper knowing of love for Jesus. These words are always spoken to my heart with Jesus' love for me; I am shown great peace in this transforming union of love. Especially in these last two chapters, I refer to words or truths that Jesus shows me—it is always in the context of union of love and peace in the Lord. Here is a poem inspired in me by the Lord that expresses the intimacy of his love for all people.

A Resolve to Love God

To embrace God
in our tears
in our joy
in our laughter
as we hear the command
to love God with all of our might.

I extend my blessings in grace
like a lava flowing through my heart
sinking into the depth of my skin
eradicating all debris of sin
where new birth
is nourished in the Creator's elements
in wondrous love.

---

4 Kieran Kavanaugh, O.D.D., and Otilio Rodriguez, O.C.D., Translators, *The Collected Works of St. John of the Cross* (Washington, D.C.: ICS Publications, Institute of Carmelite Studies, 1991).

*Emissions of gas from the earth
molten lava is the Holy Spirit gift within
steam atops craters
spewing sparks of life
of love fiery red
going nowhere
rising with a plume of love
burns in the heart in the one giving blessings.*

*Volcanic ash layers rescinded to the earth below
give rise to a new day.
God's way climbs ecstasies of the heart
with smoke rising in an ash plume
settling back into the earth
where God provides new life.*

*Home is where the heart lies open to God's love
crying no longer
laughing at infinite possibilities
not yet considered.*

*Crevices in the skin mark the lines of aging.
Crevices in the heart mark the sign of God's love
plummets sins once dormant
exploding in thunderous acts of God
who rises all sin and debris of sin
higher than plummets of ash
that rescind to the earth.*

*Rekindled is the fire of the Holy Spirit
beneath one's feet
the ground opens up
consumed by the Holy Spirit
the feet go nowhere
leveling of the ground
to coincide with temperament of
being one with Christ
oozing with eager blessings for another
alive with passion not to be rescinded
even by a volcano
for ash rescinds—
the human spirit does not.*

St. John of the Cross communicates his understanding of the intimacy in uniting with God's love in *The Living Flame of Love*.

> *O living flame of love!*
> *that tenderly wounds my soul*
> *in its deepest center! Since*
> *now you are not oppressive,*
> *now consummate! If it be your will:*
> *tear through the veil of this sweet encounter!*

We each long for this eternal love that burns deep within our soul—a flame leads one deeper inward to the most tender center of the soul. In John's commentary about the Living Flame of Love, he writes that the highest degree of perfection one can reach in this life is transformation in God.[5] I believe that the healing paradigm of Transformation of the Heart is a healing journey to transformation in God.

In the fulfillment of love, we sometimes are given the gift from the Lord to experience our love being divinely received, and we may sense that we witness a glimpse of the glory of God. It is in the unknown mystery—whether we experience it or not—that we trust, we love, and we give all of who we are to the Lord as our faith and desire to love are lit. These are words inspired in my heart by the Lord: "Give to me your love, dear child—I touch you with tenderness and take your love for my own."

Nothing more beautifully teaches us of God's invitation to open our heart to receive his love as The Spiritual Canticle written by St. John of the Cross; here are selected stanzas:

> *13. Return, dove,*
> *the wounded stag*
> *is in sight on the hill,*
> *cooled by the breeze of your flight.*
>
> *22. The bride has entered*
> *the sweet garden of her desire,*
> *and she rests in delight,*
> *laying her neck*
> *on the gentle arms of her*
> *Beloved.*

---

5 Kieran Kavanaugh, O.D.D., and Otilio Rodriguez, O.C.D., Translators, *The Collected Works of St. John of the Cross* (Washington, D.C.: ICS Publications, Institute of Carmelite Studies, 1991).

> 23. Beneath the apple tree:
> there I took you for my own,
> there I offered you my hand,
> and restored you,
> where your mother was
> corrupted.
>
> 27. There he gave me his breast;
> there he taught me a sweet and
> living knowledge;
> and I gave myself to him,
> keeping nothing back,
> there I promised to be his bride.

In the poetry of the spousal marriage with our Beloved, we surrender with all of our depth to the will of God the Father. Nothing matters but letting go of all else that exists.

In my heart and mind, the wounded stag is the Lord who reaches out for your hand, your love—and desires to experience your love, not like a drop of water, but more like rivers of love to quench his thirst, satisfy his hunger. I sense at times that I am held against the Lord's breast and know his abiding presence of love that has taken me past my sins, past my fears. I trust that I am the bride of Christ (not due to my goodness but due to the Lord's goodness) in this moment of union—we never leave one another altogether, but return to one another. The flight is the Holy Spirit in me blessing those I pray for. This love is in all, poured out as the Holy Spirit in each soul conceived.

> Jesus answered him, "Those who love me will keep my word, and my Father will love them, and we will come to them and make our home with them" (John 14:23).

You know you are in union with God's love when you embrace with the Lord Jesus, experience the sweet knowledge that you each desire one another's love, and are drawn to one another without regard for anything else. This love is united for all time. Once again, St. John of the Cross captures an aspect of eternal presence.

> 38. There you will show me
> What my soul has been seeking,
> And then you will give me,
> You, my life, will give me there
> What you gave me on that other day.

In my heart, this last line "What you gave me on that other day" means to kiss, to love, to touch and know the gentleness of the Lord, now and forever. All that is left to say is: Glory be to the Father, the Son, and the Holy Spirit. Amen.

St. Therese of Lisieux, even at the early age of her teens and 20s, knew the heart of Christ and was so drawn to Jesus' love that she wrote, "The divine call was so urgent, I would have plunged through flames to follow Jesus." She had gained comfort in her life by reading the works of St. John of the Cross. I read and re-read the writings of both St. Therese and St. John of the Cross; I find comfort in their heart's knowing of the heart of Christ. She quotes St. John of the Cross in her autobiography:

> *I have neither guide nor light, except that which shone within my heart and that guided me more surely than the midday sun to the place where He who knew me well awaited me.*[6]

St. Therese's words remind me of what I know about Jesus' love. The desire to love Jesus, as I know it, is the meaning of human existence—for the purpose of forgiveness of sins and eternal love and life.

I am drawn to two scriptures that uncover the enormity of God's love in leading us to the fulfillment of love in our heart and soul.

> *When God finished speaking with Moses on Mount Sinai,*
> *he gave him the two tablets of the covenant,*
> *tablets of stone, written with the finger of God* (Exod 31:18).

> *A new heart I will give you, and a new spirit I will put within you;*
> *and I will remove from your body the heart of stone and give you a heart of flesh* (Ezek 36:26).

---

6 John Beevers, Translator, *The Autobiography of St. Therese of Lisieux: The Story of a Soul* (New York: Image Books/Doubleday, 2001).

I saw the connection between these scriptures in prayer. I sensed Jesus' fingertips touch mine with a most tender love of the Mother and the Father, as these words were burned in my heart "little heart of Christ." I was absolutely in awe of the tenderness of the Lord's love—once again, knowing this love is for all. In the first scripture, the tablet of stone is inscribed by the finger of God—God's finger is both an obvious tool and an image of the law being given to the world with tender, divine love. In Ezekiel, we are given a new heart and our heart of stone is removed, meaning God has washed clean our old self, our heart, and renewed us in the waters of Baptism. God desires for each person to experience the tenderness of this love, and the completion of our heart's journey to God. I believe that for those who are not baptized, God reaches even deeper with grace. All are welcome to the heart of Christ.

The Kingdom of Heaven is Now

We each are invited to the Kingdom of Heaven grace now. The entryway to the Kingdom is not through the eye of a needle, but with "the ear of the heart" as St. Benedict teaches us in his 6th century monastic rule.[7] The Rule of St. Benedict, practiced worldwide in Benedictine monastic communities, contains numerous references to returning to the heart in all affairs and preferring nothing to the love of Christ.

As an Oblate of the Order of St. Benedict, I was asked to choose the name of a saint. I asked for the name Benedict because St. Benedict calls us to prefer nothing to the heart of Christ and to always show a heart of hospitality—to love the Lord and to love others. My deepest yearning is to love Jesus. To deepen my love and faith, I participate in oblate retreats or personal retreats several times a year at St. Benedict's Abbey and Seminary in Mount Angel, Oregon.

Here is a personal healing story that occurred at the abbey, where Jesus drew me to the "fulfillment of love" moments of divine union, what I felt was the absolute knowing of eternal life—where I also came to better see my purpose to serve the Lord. As the heart is centered in God's love, we are drawn by the Lord to a depth of love and concern for all others.

---

7 *The Rule of St. Benedict* (Collegeville, MN: Liturgical Press, 1982).

I arrived at the abbey on a stormy evening, somehow feeling inadequate to do "healing hands" prayers that I had become accustomed to doing with little strain. I hurried to the chapel and approached the Blessed Sacrament for prayer, seeking assistance and reassurance from Jesus. How was it that I could pray with my hands on anyone, and make any difference? Had not the Lord been teaching me all along to trust in his love and to surrender to the will of God the Father? Did I matter and did my prayer matter? In my weakness, I felt inadequate in my own calling.

As I knelt down before the Blessed Sacrament, I was greeted with a huge clap of thunder that shook the walls, followed by more lightning and rain—and at the same time I felt an inner peace of having just arrived home. I laughed to myself; being struck by lightning didn't appear likely. My prayer began with a question: Can I do this kind of prayer and is it pleasing to God? God's answer in my heart was yes, because God always leads such prayers. I was, in each instance, to show up with love in my heart and a deep surrender to God's will and God the Father's strength.

Kneeling before the Blessed Sacrament, I knew the words in my heart as clear as day: "I am afraid. I am alone." I sensed that Jesus was speaking of his own heart, and I could see my heart as well. I recalled the times in my life when this was true, and reflected with gratitude on the moment when these words held the most significance to me. I realized God was showing me the depth of my wounds so that I would have compassion for all the others for whom I would be called to pray. Being filled with self-doubt and humbled by my own knowing of suffering, I turned to—or was drawn to—God the Father's love. The prayer was filled with grace and beauty, and I felt blessed for the work that lay ahead in the hours to come.

A few hours later, I returned to the Blessed Sacrament to pray. Soon, new words were written on my heart: "I am hungry. No one feeds me." These words were in the center of the Eucharist. The Lord spoke to me of his hunger for my love and for the love of all of humanity. How is it that we can fully love the Lord Jesus Christ? As the Lord has rivers of love for each one of us, our heart contains a river of love for the Lord. The Lord's love extends to all people through the Eucharist so that sins may be forgiven. The Lord's hunger is for love from each of us so that the fullest reconciliation of sin can be achieved—the Lord thirsts for our wellness in body, mind, spirit, and soul. In our heart's desire to love the Lord, the Lord's thirst or desire to receive our love is quenched.

Then, more words: "I give you the golden heart of Christ—use it."

My sense of gratitude to God for my own healing and for knowing the heart of Christ was profound. I felt a renewed sense of peace, and the grace to pray in surrender to God's will.

I grew in my confidence to pray, remembering how often I had witnessed the "golden heart of Christ"—the great beauty and strength of his love. I simply had to pray in the way I had been taught, remembering that God the Father's will was at play, and that my role was in fact a simple one as long as I remembered to receive and give love.

The next morning, following Mass, I was outside the church waiting for my friend for whom I was to do a healing prayer—when I noticed a toddler balancing precariously on the edge of a two-foot bench; his older brother had nearly knocked him off onto the brick floor. I moved in close enough to catch him if necessary; by now he was about to cry. I knelt down and asked his brother, who was about 4, to help him. The older boy wrapped his arms around his baby brother, kissed him on the cheek, and then asked the toddler for a kiss. It was so sweet. Then he said, "I kissed him because he is my favorite baby." They kissed each other's cheeks back and forth three times. My mothering instinct was ignited by the Holy Spirit—and I sensed the Blessed Mother loved each of her children. I felt moved by grace to reflect on the siblings' exchange of love. God wishes for us to see love in all; he asks for nothing more. My heart was united quickly with the love of God the Father. This very simple love and care-taking of one another is the way to arrive at God's doorstep hand in hand with the Lord.

I was aware that preparation for the prayer with my friend had clearly begun. I was no longer feeling alone or hesitant. My love for the Lord, in these moments, was clear to me as I surrendered to God's desire to love me. The Lord drew me to love, and I surrendered. In each instance where I know God's love, it is never for me alone, but for all people—God has infinite love for all. Soon after, my friend arrived, and we walked to our place of prayer. I shared my story and my "mother" love for these little ones, and he spoke about grandmother love. As we arrived at our prayer room, I was calmed believing the prayer was in God's hands. Feeling the gentle presence of the Holy Spirit, we began to pray. In union with God's love, my heart soon contained great peace and a vision of a painting stretched on an easel—Jesus' grace filled the entire top half of the painting—in softness and exquisite beauty; the lower half was the condition of cancer that was also grace-filled with love of God the Father, who was gazing over my friend. We each were totally loved and embraced by God, and in these powerful moments of grace, I experienced a watershed moment in my trust of God the Father's love—and the absolute knowing that life and death are one—and that God holds both. Life and love are eternal. I believe that this same love lies within each of us.

When you experience this closeness with God the Father, nothing else holds much importance. God heals what God heals, period. I didn't even question what in my friend had been healed. I had gained wisdom and understanding. This visual and spoken prayer symbolized the complete fulfillment of love with the Lord Jesus Christ, the Father, and the Holy Spirit. I knew without a doubt that the grace of the Kingdom of Heaven is available to us on earth.

To be fully present on earth, we need to be willing to see the light of God following our earthly life not as something to fear, but as love to embrace. My faith is that Jesus' merciful love is for each person alike, and that if we seek forgiveness and truth in our heart, we will be drawn to divine union of love. I trust that love that was not perfect on earth is made so in heaven. Observing a glimpse of the Kingdom of Heaven grace on earth is one thing, yet none of us have an understanding of the glory of the Kingdom of Heaven that awaits us. What would it look like if all people turned toward love, all of the time? Jesus excludes no one, ever. If you desire to love Jesus, you can find the fulfillment of love on earth and know it is also eternal.

There are many forms of existence on the planet—the walking dead, the person alive whose heart is centered in Christ, and those who are fulfilled by the love of the Lord Jesus Christ who have surrendered their will to God's will.

As I receive Jesus' tender and merciful love, my heart responds with words of poetry. Jesus inspired my heart and Spirit with these words of love and healing.

Encounter with Jesus Christ

Into the caverns of my love
I behold you, child of Jesus.
With knowledge of sin and release of sin
you receive my love,
blessing all who you are.

Bathed in the mysteries of God's eternal love
with blood cleansing even your organs
supplanted by the love of God—
Is there anything you wish for that you don't have?

This ecstasy of love is my desire
to abide in your soul
for the healing of others.

The soul of the Lord Jesus Christ
bears love onto your soul
consuming you in holy flames of love.

The eternal love of God
is the gift of the Holy Spirit
in the womb of Christ
of creation itself.

We know the absolute fulfillment of love with the Lord can only be known upon our death. But the Lord has shown many people through the ages a rapture of love, his heart freely given out. The experience of rapture is an instance when we know we are in the presence of divine love, as it is infinitely more powerful than human love, and we recognize it as pure love. God shows many people ecstasies of love or "rapture," a spontaneous depth knowing of love for the Lord—an experience beyond human love, and perhaps a glimpse of the fulfillment of God's love in the Kingdom. The rapture of the heart is so powerful it can never be mistaken for anything other than God's love, and has been illustrated by many mystics through thousands of years.

Nothing is obtained from God except by love. Once the heart is awakened, it returns often to the Lord to worship, to praise God, and to love. To fully love the Lord (as in a raptured state of being), there is a clear awareness that the heart is attached to nothing but God's love. This is the meaning of surrender to the Lord's love, the Lord's will, the Lord's truth, the Lord's beauty.

The following poems were inspired in my heart by the Lord. I gave my heart to God, my will and desire to be one with God eternally. Grace filled every nook and cranny of my body. This rapture happened in prayer over an hour's time, as God took me deeper and deeper into the caverns of his love. He was in no hurry. The beauty, peace, and joy of holy love are indescribable. I knew the entire time that this was God's love for all of humanity, and this display of love to me was for the sake of all people—my surrender to God's will.

While Jesus displays his love to me, I am without any other desires other than to love Jesus and be in His presence. As I received this poetry into my heart through the Holy Spirit, I was motionless and seemingly with just a whisper of breath.

A Raptured Heart

Kindled love
Penetrating my soul
Longing for Jesus Christ
Who touches my entire being
In one sweep of a brush
I am colored red
For the blood of Christ
Has risen in me
My heart transformed
Painted a new image of Christ
Risen and healed
For the sake of the One Body
All are healed
Kiss, touch, tender witness
Of my love
Draws your heart deeper to touch
Not of a distant God
Jesus close to the heart
You sink deeper into the mysteries of my love
Your heart is content; nothing else matters
God is in no hurry to leave his child of Jesus.

*Pray for all to know Jesus' love
is what I desire from you
in fullness of Jesus' presence.
You are the Bride of Christ
kissed and held for eternity—given to me your heart of love.*

Final Earthly Desire

*Oh sweetest desire
of Christ in you
receive deeper yet
an angel's dusting of love,
showers from above
in mystical union
is captured a tenderness
of Christ's longing
for your soul's presence.*

*Heaven is union,
communion
of the fullest sense
the Eucharist
touching heaven and the human soul
as one
carries the soul at death to the
Kingdom
whose final desire is
the kiss of God.*

The Lord Jesus Christ is the guardian of my heart. In the shelter of Jesus' wisdom, I have gained far more than I could have foreseen in my lifetime. With my desire to love him, I am given the way to share with others what I have gained. This has happened through my heart by grace; I am given the freedom and peace to love and a desire to surrender to God's will in all things. I wake up each morning and greet Jesus with love and joy in my heart.

We cannot know the fulfillment of love until the moment of death, when the Lord takes us to the Kingdom of Heaven. However, through grace we find glimpses of the Kingdom while we are yet on the earth. In grace, Jesus shows us the inner beauty of another soul, and glimpses of the beauty of our own soul. These glimpses of the ecstasy of God's love and our union with God's love, as shown to us by the Holy Spirit, lead us to our soul's longing for completion with the Lord. I find not only the beauty of the Lord's love and presence, but hope in eternal life—through these glimpses of the Kingdom of Heaven's grace.

"Love Set Free" is another poem that is my heart's response to Jesus' love for me. Experiencing the freedom in my heart to love others has become a common experience in prayer—it is all gift in the Lord's grace.

Love Set Free: The Heart's Possession in Christ

Her heart is touched
by petals of a flower
with the softness
of the Lord's gift of love—
the Holy Spirit.

The pronounced adoration of love
for the Lord Jesus is heard
with trumpets blowing
music pierces the skies
in a funnel of love
touching down on all life.

Her Beloved's kiss
a gentle whisper of love
touches all in sight.
While the heart's joy is caressed inside out
the Divine touch
gently fans a breeze outward.

Her love is in His possession.
The Lord proclaims his little spirit of Jesus
His bride of Christ
risen from sin
now resting against her Beloved's breast
where she wishes to reside longer.

As the dove's wings touch down
in reverence to God the Father
a dusting in her hair is felt and
his tender whisper of love
is heard throughout her being.
She is drawn by his prowess
to the Lord's desire within.

*Knowing her tongue once was twisted
her speech is now made clear
as she hears the music of the Lord's heart
trumpets resound in unison upon enlightened others.
His tender kiss is upon her.*

*She surrenders into her Beloved's molded heart.
In the distance the night's breeze
comes upon her for time unmarked.
With more garlands of love
His poem is sung to her in a splendor of love.*

*His joy and kiss is the wisdom of the Lord
who preaches love for all
denounces all sin
and lifts her to witness eternal life.*

In my heart's receipt of this poem "The Birth of Christ," my entire being was made still, held in God's grace and in the divinity of God's love in all of creation. I witnessed the nutrients in the earth, creation itself that is for all of humankind.

The Birth of Christ

*Drumming
the beat of desire.
All love is born.
All sin is lost
to the wind—
in the Holy Spirit's rising—
the Son.*

*Kindled love afire
is your heart's desire.
Renewal of touch
leads a heart once astray
to the home and hearth of
the Lord Jesus Christ.*

Jesus' heart was a heart of divine truth, always seeking the will of God the Father. Jesus, incarnate, always lived in truth. As humans, we constantly seek the truth of our heart in prayer and pray for intercession so that we and others may be healed. Jesus lived in truth. There was shared love between Jesus and his Father. Perhaps the fulfillment of love in the Kingdom of Heaven is where we, too, will live eternally in union with God's love and desiring only God's will. There will be no more stumbling.

> *Then Jesus said to the Jews who had believed in him,*
> *"If you continue in my word, you are truly my disciples;*
> *and you will know the truth,*
> *and the truth will make you free"* (John 8:31-32).

So, how is it that we are led to the fulfillment of love? The real culprit of all healing needs has its root in the need for forgiveness. The Holy Spirit is wisdom and love, the depth of which guides our heart toward deliverance from sin. People who seek forgiveness from sin are those who know the longing to love Jesus. Many of the faithful today may not seek love to un-root sin, but to forget sins of the past. The purpose of seeking love and seeking forgiveness is to un-root sins that may be lengthy patterns of one's lifestyle.

The real culprit of all healing needs has its root in the need for forgiveness.

In the Lord's Prayer, we are taught the simple command to ask God for forgiveness of ourselves, and to seek forgiveness of those who have wounded us. It is good to add "all that is known and unknown to us," because we forget a great deal. Jesus waits until we are ready and listens to our needs for forgiveness. We are never turned away.

To be human is to experience loss and to experience love. All loss can be captured in forgiveness prayers with God. This draws one to the eternal love and presence of God to be spoken and seen in one's heart. Eternal wisdom of love is love that is eternal, where all are united with the One Body of Christ and the One Body is healed in prayer and in Sacrament. In this healing, one comes to know a sense of the purity of love in the heart, and then turns to give real blessings to others. That is the simplicity of the gift of the Holy Spirit in me—to give blessings to others, blessings in union with Jesus' love. I have learned many lessons of love as the Lord has led me in the journey toward purity of heart, Transformation of the Heart in Christ's love. Why is this needed today? The human condition, especially today, has many competing interests that result in the burying of sin. It is simply easier to look the other way in many instances. Transformation of the Heart is about how and why to surrender to

Jesus' love for the forgiveness of sins.

The gift of the Holy Spirit as "truth" is present in each and every heart today, yet the heart's capacity to give and receive love—and in that union of love, to find the heart's wisdom of truth—is what is missing in some people today. We do not reach the fulfillment of love without truth.

We do not reach the fulfillment of love without truth.

The Holy Spirit is the eternal flame of love—the breath of Christ passing over you. This is both life everlasting and love everlasting.

Chapter Eleven

A Glimpse of the Kingdom of Heaven

Love has so worked within me that it has transformed my soul into itself.[1] St. Therese of Lisieux

As we open to the presence of Christ's heart and offer works of charity to others, we sometimes are given knowledge and a glimpse of God's eternal presence of love and the Kingdom of Heaven grace that is at hand for all people. When this happens, it is not a sign of preferential treatment by God to one person or another, yet it is a gift of discernment of spirit and wisdom to be witnessed for the sake of the Kingdom. Jesus invites each and every soul to this kind of transformation—this is the hope of everlasting love, eternal life in the fullness of God's love. Language does not do justice to such moments of grace because there is far greater mystery than any knowing, yet my heart was filled with peace, love, and a knowing that even a glimpse of the Kingdom of Heaven grace is beyond any typical human experience of love.

---

1 John Beevers, Translator, *The Autobiography of St. Therese of Lisieux: The Story of a Soul* (New York: Image Books/Doubleday, 2001).

Transformation of the Heart healing encapsulates steps of personal release and surrender, growth in personal and universal wisdom, and the deep grace of going beyond ourselves as we open fully to God's love. This chapter includes a short story and poem that illustrate the profound grace that enlightened my spirit to witness a beatific vision of the heart of Christ as an eternal blessing of love. God calls all people to purity of heart, and purity of heart was given to me as a gift of the Lord in this vision of the Kingdom. I trust that in my glimpse of this grace, there is much greater mystery left of what the Kingdom of Heaven is really like—that no one will know until their death and being Risen in Jesus' love.

> *The Sixth Beatitude: Blessed are the pure of heart, for they will see God* (Matt 5:8).

What is the experience of one who is shown by God a glimpse of the grace of purity of heart, and does this only come after great conversion of sin? This is by God's goodness, not by our goodness. My understanding is that the grace of purity of heart is freedom from the deceit of the heart—and this is necessary before full conversion. Unless we are dead, we have not yet "arrived" to the fullness of purity of heart that will be ours in the Kingdom of Heaven. Yet our hearts are made pure for the moment in grace. As I witnessed a sense of purity of heart in myself in grace, I knew without a doubt that the Kingdom of Heaven was for me, too. It is for all of course, yet I felt as certain as anything that it was mine, and I trusted that God's plan in every aspect of my life had been to lead me there and in my prayer life, to pray for the gift of eternal life for all.

God's grace is always given freely, never earned, so we are never to consider ourselves complete in our conversion from sin until the time of death. Seeing Christ at the time of death is both absolute conversion from sin and a personal escort to the Kingdom of Heaven. Any spiritual or mystical prayer visits to the Kingdom prior to death are simply grace that is God's gift given freely, and, if anything, we receive more humility with this gift—we understand that it is all Christ's doing, not our own. Beatific visions of Christ are simple and beautiful expressions of God's love—they inform us with a glimpse of what the Kingdom of Heaven holds for us upon our death.

In God's love, we come to know that deceit of our heart is lifted and that God's love is truth, peace, and reconciliation from sin. We welcome this union with God's love as a foreshadowing of what we can expect in the Kingdom—and the rest lies in the mystery of God's love that is healing to the body, mind, spirit, and soul.

Another way to reflect on a beatific vision is that Christ carries a person's awareness to "oneness with God," where you feel that you exist in Christ—nothing on earth is in your awareness, only absolute love. We should never desire to be God—that is the opposite of what the prayer life is—yet when God carries us to the Kingdom of Heaven, we come into the fullness of the presence of God, at least a glimpse of it.

As I pray in union with God's love, there are times when I feel Jesus' grief, and I know that Jesus wept for all sinners. Yet it is not this knowing that Jesus calls me to; we do not pray so that we can carry the wounds of Christ, but so that we can acknowledge that Jesus suffered and died for all sins, and give up our own suffering. It is important to always know the line between self and God; we may be carried to a beatific vision, but trying to be in a beatific vision is not pleasing to God.

I was carried to a beatific vision and experienced a release of my own suffering and loss. My understanding and my words about this experience are less than accurate or clear, but I believe that God had a purpose that was beyond my understanding. The Lord drew me to this experience. I desired for Jesus to release my suffering, and the Lord responded by raising me to the Kingdom of Heaven, to his presence. When I pray today, if I begin to experience sorrow, I pray immediately for the Lord to show me only his love and to help me let go of whatever sorrow is mine. I draw a line so that I don't experience the sufferings of anyone else. In the face of suffering, I pray for the healing of the One Body of Christ for the sake of the Kingdom of Heaven. I believe that many souls are touched by Christ in each prayer. This is mostly mystery, yet I feel that many people have been healed.

In *The Sanctifier*, his classic work on the Holy Spirit, Archbishop Luis Martinez writes about purity of heart as one being without need for the earth. The Greeks had a word to describe this idea of holiness: *hagios*, meaning "without earth." To be pure is to be without earth; that is, to be free of all that is not God. This was my experience during the beatific vision of Christ described below—I knew only love with no boundaries or edges. It was as if I was lifted away from the earth and then returned. In God's grace, I knew I had not been made perfect, but that I had witnessed the Kingdom of Heaven as perfect love—and in this I knew the truth of God's love in me and in my life. God is very pleased with our love given to him.

As you read this chapter, I invite you to open your heart to truth and to wisdom in your own heart, and consider the possibilities of divine union of love with the Lord Jesus Christ for all time—eternity. This love is not beyond anyone's grasp, yet oftentimes there is work of the heart that awaits a person. The capacity to grow in love with the Lord Jesus Christ lies in trusting in God's love and gaining trust in one's own heart of love for Jesus.

The capacity to grow in love with the Lord Jesus Christ lies in trusting in God's love and gaining trust in one's own heart of love for Jesus.

The Beatific Vision—Jesus' gift of presence

On the day of this blessed event that stretched me beyond all my knowing of love, I had awakened feeling discouraged. I was not welcome in a particular place of worship and felt sad about the ways I had been rejected by three people whom I loved. In their rejection, something important had been taken from me, and the experience was heavy in my heart. I began the prayer as I do each day, praying over the Gospel. There was a surprise gift for me in this Gospel reading. I was familiar with this scripture, but had never quite heard it the way I did on this particular morning.

> Now as they went on their way, he entered a certain village, where a woman named Martha welcomed him into her home. She had a sister named Mary, who sat at the Lord's feet and listened to what he was saying. But Martha was distracted by her many tasks; so she came to him and asked,
> "Lord, do you not care that my sister has left me to do all the work by myself? Tell her then to help me."
> But the Lord answered her,
> "Martha, Martha, you are worried and distracted by many things;

there is need of only one thing. Mary has chosen the better part, which will not be taken away from her" (Luke 10:38-42).

In my reading of this Scripture, I spoke to Jesus as the last two sentences struck my heart and I was brought to tears of joy: "You are so good, Lord Jesus Christ! You do not take what is important from me; you leave me eternally with my love for you and my desire to love you. I am grateful for your teachings to me and for your merciful love, Jesus. Thanks be to God. Praise be to you Lord Jesus Christ."

I heard Jesus' words to me: "Do not hide your love from yourself or from them, dear daughter, love with all of your heart." Then I was drawn to God's love in grace for a very long time, more than thirty minutes, where I consented to love each with all of my heart and I prayed for the souls of the ones who had harmed me; Jesus inspired these words in my heart: "A blessing of the eternal is upon you, dear daughter; let be in God's arms of love for you, a further blessing that you are so loved is upon you in the depth of God's arms of love; surrender to God's will once again and know you are so loved by the Lord Jesus Christ."

> *"You are so good, Lord Jesus Christ! You do not take what is important from me; you leave me eternally with my love for you and my desire to love you."*

In this moment, I believed that I was so loved, and my own desire to worship and to love the Lord was absolutely intact. I was raised by Jesus in this perfect truth, and I could want nothing more. Tears of gratitude streamed down my face, and I knew that Jesus' presence was upon me. I surrendered and let go into Jesus' arms, giving him my heart to hold, trusting in his love for me; I rested "one with God."

Jesus' teaching to me in this moment was that I was experiencing salvation grace—it was in me and through me for the sake of the Kingdom, for the healing of the One Body of Christ, the Church, and for the forgiveness of sins in myself and others. I felt I was taken out of my physical body to a place where I did not need the earth. I was raised in his love with a sense of absolute freedom. My desire to love Jesus was made complete, I was absolutely surrendered, and I let go of the earth as I knew it.

In a cocoon of love, I witnessed an image that was all red, all moist, all joy, all love . . . all eternal and yet only a glimpse of what was to come upon death. I did not hold back from Jesus' touch, his intimacy of love abounded in every part of me. I was suspended in time and in air, my love being pulled forward like a torch that contained the brightest of all light as well as a hint of light. I was surrendered into what it must be like when one dies—nothing is needed on the earth and all is provided for in the Kingdom. I am aware that these words are not nearly enough to describe this union with God.

In this depth of love, I saw an image of the altar at Mount Angel Abbey, symbolizing that I would never be without a parish home. Then I saw an image of St. Benedict with these words written below his image: "My heart sings with praise, for his love is for me, too."

I was filled with joy and knew that I was called to this grace of absolute knowing that Jesus loved me. Nothing else was important. Then the words: "Jesus as pen" . . . showed me that it is Jesus who directs my pen.

I saw a glimpse of heaven, yet when I die, I believe that I will see much more of the Glory of God the Father. At the completion of this grace-filled prayer, Christ asked me to "love one another on earth and to recognize Christ in one and in all."

When our heart is made pure, even for a second, we know the most powerful love of Christ for us—the beatific vision of the Kingdom. My calling is to pray for others to open their heart to know the love of Christ and to receive the grace of purity of heart. When we pray, God's grace is present in the other; yet it is up to the other how they respond to grace. God waits. I am called to teach people about God's love and to invite them to pay attention to God in them.

The philosopher and theologian Thomas Aquinas, in his writings in *Summa Contra Gentile*,[2] offers this belief:

> *Thus only the fullness of the Beatific Vision satisfies this fundamental desire of the human soul to know God.*

Perhaps it is God's will to draw many hearts to the beatific vision, to the Kingdom of Heaven grace. We all await the real presence of Christ. As my heart is drawn to the desire to love Jesus, I consent to receive the grace of ecstatic union, and in this grace, a deep burn-

---

2 Thomas Aquinas, *Summa Contra Gentile*, Chapter XLIX.

ing desire to love the Lord is made known to me. The beatific vision, as I experienced it, was in some sense the completion of that burning desire. With only a glimpse of the Kingdom of Heaven, I could see the difference between earth and the Kingdom of Heaven. In heaven, one simply does not need the earth, yet is fully present to the earth in spirit. Love is absolute, and there are no edges to this love; it is divine unity and communion in God. My journey to receive these graces has been through my heart's journey to understand God's love. I did not earn this grace—it is all gift and holds a purpose in God's eyes that perhaps I will not understand until my death. This is my experience in Christ, and I believe the purpose is for the healing of the One Body of Christ, the Church.

When I felt my presence returned to the earth in grace, I received this poem through my heart; it speaks a depth of God's love to me that may or may not be seen by others. I experience joy and love each time I read it. I gave thanks to Jesus for touching me in his eternal grace.

A Beatific Vision

*Twinings of love forever sacred
is Jesus' heart all red
displayed to me.
Oh soft and moist is my own love
indescribable union—
my yearning fulfilled.*

*In oneness
I am so loved by Christ
of nothing else shall I want
of nothing else shall I pray—
but for all peoples to know oneness with Christ's love.*

*In shapes of love beyond diamonds
Christ immerses my senses.
I am in mid air—
where all are one—
the eternal soul is risen
with no need for the earth
the Kiss of the Holy Spirit is made complete.*

*Yearnings to love made pure.
Enlightenment*

*beyond my reach
is all of God's Kingdom
embracing me from all sides
edges not found
only oneness with Christ.*

*The color red
blurring away—not really seen
I sink ever more
not hidden
but made brilliant
in the illumined spirit of God.*

*Ever present gift of the Holy Spirit
glistening the color of white
in brilliant love
beyond the purest diamonds
too bright to display—
this kind of love
Jesus gives out to all the world.*

*Suspended in mid air
is for all
in the midst of the love of the Lord Jesus Christ.
Not a burning bush
but a bushel of adoration of Christ
lifted to the Kingdom of Heaven.*

*Immersion of love
lies promise of Eternal Kingdom
where all is made clear—
Wisdom is
oneness with Christ's love.*

*All knowledge is in the heart
of God's love poured forth
through the Holy Spirit.
Never alone but always one with God
is your immersion with Christ the Savior.*

*Purity of love
only words dear child
of a heart transformed into Christ
—is oneness with Christ
Of this is purity of heart of love
God's gift of presence is upon you.*

Why did the Lord draw my heart and soul to this experience? I believe it was because I needed it for my salvation. I witnessed an instance of my own suffering lifted. I did not earn it. I was given this grace. I trust that what is in this grace—the Lord's eternal love—is for all people. I had been praying for those who did great harm to me, and I know for certain now that there is great benefit to praying for those who hurt us. The question for each of us, perhaps, is what can we offer to God today? We each are more alike than different, in that we need to be set free from our sins and those committed against us. God awaits our love and acknowledgement of our suffering, and the suffering of the One Body of Christ. I have let go to God a great deal of suffering in my faith journey, and I have known loneliness beyond what I'd like to admit. I am grateful for the many lessons of God's love. The Holy Spirit in me is the same Holy Spirit in each and every person, and God's love is the same for each of us. This experience brought me humility of spirit, not a sense of perfection in myself but a sense of perfection in God's presence and love.

A word on the teaching of Christ in my heart about the words given to me: "My heart sings with praise, for his love is for me, too." Jesus asks us each to hold in our heart as we pray, the intention and absolute belief that Jesus' love is for us, too, and to bathe in this love as Jesus draws our heart in union with his. This intention of presence is part of the prayer practice itself; believing and trusting in God's love for us is necessary for everyone to be healed from brokenness. In addition to knowing God's grace is flowing in prayers, I acknowledge that Jesus' love is for me—and in this, the most pure form of human love can be united with Christ's love for the sake of the Kingdom. Both are necessary. If everyone participated in their faith by believing that God's love was for them, too, the fighting in the world just might stop. This one belief leads the heart to love God, and to find the truth of our deepest desire, which is to love Jesus and to love and take care of one another. This can lead us to reconciliation with God and one another, and to peace.

Archbishop Luis Martinez describes the soul's experience when it witnesses Christ:[3]

---

[3] Archbishop Luis M. Martinez, *The Sanctifier: The Classic Work on the Holy Spirit* (Boston: Pauline Books and Media, 2003).

> *Who can explain what the soul experiences when it beholds the Beloved rising in the midst of the shadows that change into light. It is the Beloved, but so great, so beautiful, so irresistible, so divine, that the soul seems to see him for the first time. It is the same One to whom it gave itself utterly—but it did not even suspect the beauty of his face, the sun of his glance, the heaven of his smile, the ocean of his goodness, the abyss of his love. Mortal powers cannot bear to contemplate such beauty—an ecstasy so intense as that which the divine vision produces does not belong in the fragile vase of the human heart. The soul faints before the mighty invasion of light and love. These apparitions are rapid and fleeting, because the natural weakness of the soul could not support them. The Beloved goes away leaving in the soul the fire of charity and the ardor of desire. He returns again, filling the soul with such celestial delights that it knows its anxieties and its sacrifices were nothing in comparison with such a reward.*

As we enter into the Kingdom of Heaven grace of God's holy presence in us—and this grace is for all of us—we may be asked to surrender beyond our knowing into the fullness of the presence of Christ for the sake of the Kingdom. In what felt like a second beatific vision of the Lord, my heart was raised and I felt Jesus say in my heart: "I take your heart for my own." This is the Kingdom of Heaven grace on earth that we are called to for the sake of others and for the Kingdom. To know this love is the profound message of this book.

At times in prayer I know what I refer to as "holy tears." I witness Jesus' suffering for the world and tears well up in my eyes—a bodily response to my love for God and my gratitude for Jesus' merciful love for all people.

> *My tears have been my food day and night, while people say to me continually, Where is your God?* (Ps 42:3).

One's soul is thirsting for God so that the desire for God can be fulfilled on earth, as it will be in heaven. To give up one's own desires for the desire of God is the key to happiness. One's own self-desires are put aside and only then can one truly find God.

Perhaps even in monastic and religious life there are many competing interests, yet one's self-desires must be given up to a large extent.

Because of our human nature, this can only happen in the depth of our surrender to the desire to love Jesus in prayer. To achieve oneness of love is each person's soul's innermost desire—and this is possible in the depth of prayer. As Thomas Aquinas says: "In all of our desires, whether we realize it or not, we are really thirsting for God."[4]

In the same way, we are called to surrender to the same depth of love for our neighbor, which includes all people, especially those who have harmed us and taken things from us, or those whom we have harmed. In this depth of love for God, we come to know something about God and we are shown our own soul—our heart can be raised in grace from the greatest of sins and rejection against us, and from the depth of our own sins. We know in oneness with Christ's love that this is healing to the One Body of Christ. The way that I understand "oneness with Christ's love" in my prayers and in my daily life, is what Fr. Thomas Keating refers to as "transforming union"— living daily life with the invincible conviction of continuous union with God's love.[5] In oneness with Christ, which is a gift from God intended for all people, God's grace flows in us and through us for all people, for the sake of the Kingdom. We may pray for one person or another, but God knows where healing is needed . . . and I believe that grace goes out to the far corners of the world. Fr. Thomas Keating in *Invitation to Love* writes, "The principal means of reaching transforming union is the personal love of Christ."[6] In God's grace, we are all united and Risen with the One Body of Christ.

I believe it is God's will for the Holy Spirit, which is present in each human being, to draw our hearts of love home to the Lord. It is my hope that this book—and particularly the Transformation of the Heart missions of love-seeking, truth-seeking, and love-sharing— has helped you open your heart and be transformed in Jesus' love. Transformation of the Heart is not only a contemplative practice, but a way toward eternal life.

---

4 Mary Ann Fatula, *Thomas Aquinas: Preacher and Friend* (Collegeville, MN: Liturgical Press, 1993).

5 Thomas Keating, *Invitation to Love: The Way of Christian Contemplation* (New York: Continuum Press, copyright by St. Benedict's Monastery, 1992).

6 Ibid.

As we desire to love the Lord and are drawn by Jesus to a depth of this desire, and then to our own truth, we become a servant in Christ's love. From the heart of Christ we are given in the fashion of love, the desire to be a servant to one another. We give all that we know to Jesus and ask only to be a servant in his love for the sake of all. Jesus washed the feet of the disciples, and surrendered to his crucifixion in obedience and love for his father—so we too should surrender in our love for the Lord. My servant way is to love the Lord and to offer prayer.

And most of all, we remember and embrace Jesus. . . .

> *For this is how God loved the world: he gave his only Son,*
> *so that everyone who believes in him may not perish*
> *but may have eternal life* (John 3:16).

About the Author

Through her love for Christ, all of Gina Anderson's work centers on the spiritual growth and healing of others. Her commitment to serving God springs from her deep Catholic faith and spiritual formation as a Benedictine Oblate at Mount Angel Abbey and Seminary, and Oblate affiliation with Calmodolese Oblates, a contemplative Benedictine community. She is pursuing national certification as a chaplain and currently works as a Resident Chaplain for St. Joe's Medical Center. Gina is pursuing a Master's in Pastoral Studies at Loyola University at Chicago, and has a prior Master's in Social Work from the University of Washington. She has a leadership background, working on systems change and bringing spirituality into mental health services. She leads contemplative retreats and holistic healing through prayer in her parish and community.

www.ingramcontent.com/pod-product-compliance
Lightning Source LLC
LaVergne TN
LVHW051645080426
835511LV00016B/2497